Essential Music Theory © 2022 by San Marco Publications. All rights reserved.

All right reserved. No part of this book may be reproduced in any form or by electronic or mechanical means including Information storage and retrieval systems without permission in writing from the author.

ISNB: 9781896499325

Contents

Lesson 1: **Scale Review**	1
Lesson 2: **The Chromatic Scale**	12
Lesson 3: **The Whole Tone Scale**	18
Lesson 4: **The Octatonic Scale**	20
Lesson 5: **The Pentatonic Scale**	22
Lesson 6: **The Blues Scale**	24
Lesson 7: **History 1**	27
Review 1	32
Lesson 8: **Intervals**	34
Lesson 9: **Rhythm and Meter**	41
Lesson 10: **Triads**	56
Lesson 11: **History 2**	65
Lesson 12: **Seventh Chords**	69
Review 2	76
Lesson 13: **Cadences**	78
Lesson 14: **Transposition**	91
Lesson 15: **Melody Writing**	99
Lesson 16: **History 3**	109
Review 3	117
Lesson 17: **Music Analysis**	120
Music Terms and Signs	128
Exam	135

1
Scale Review

The Circle of Fifths

Figure 1.1 is the circle of 5ths with major and minor keys. The *circle of 5ths* is a chart organizing all of the keys into a system that is used to relate them to one another. At the top, is the key of C major, which has no sharps or flats in its key signature. Each stop on the circle moving clockwise from C is a key with one more sharp than the previous key. Each stop moving down counter-clockwise from C is a key with one more flat than the last key.

Figure 1.1

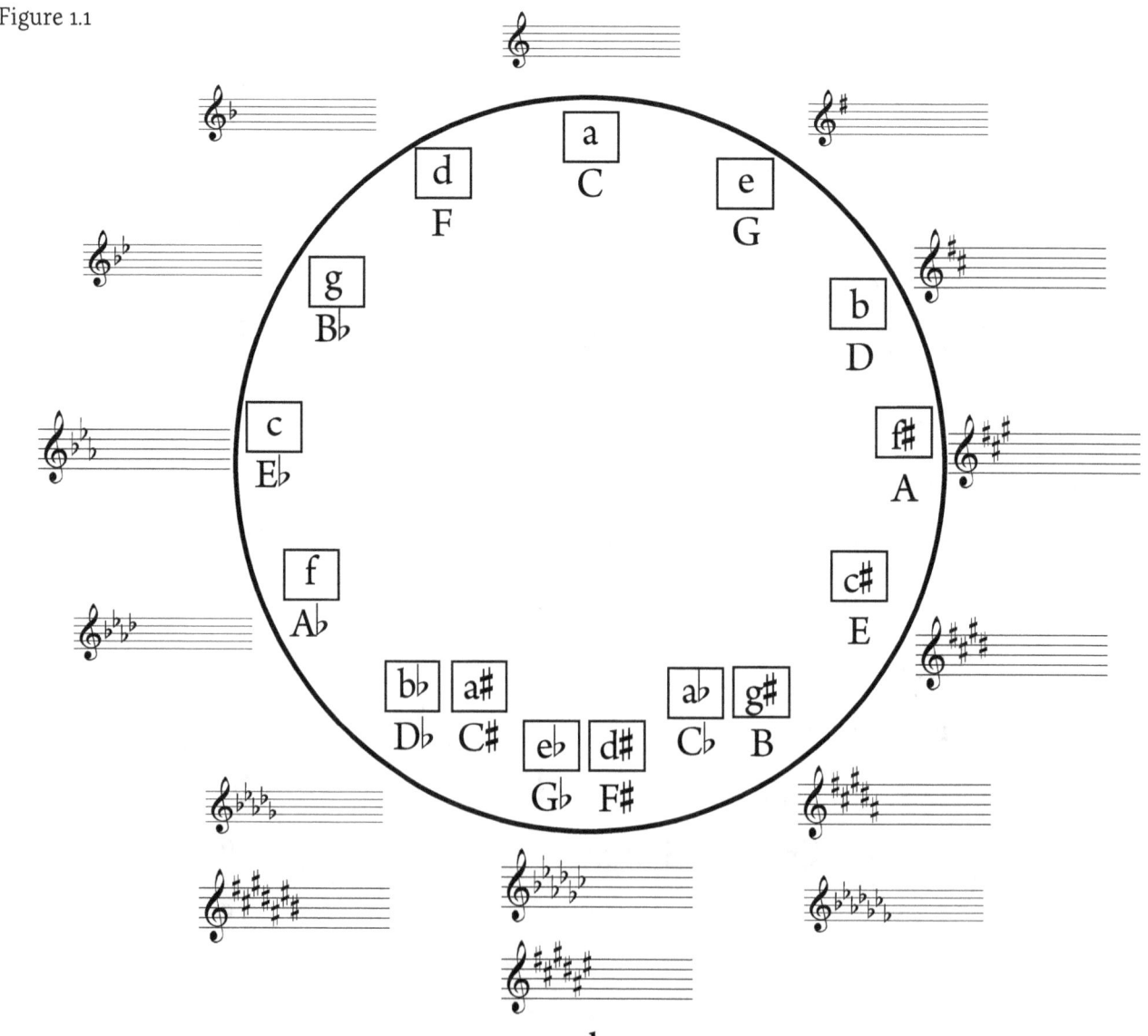

Key Signatures

Figure 1.2 shows the placement of sharps and flats on the grand staff.

Figure 1.2

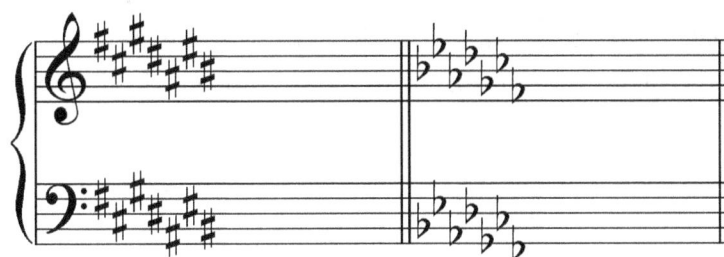

Technical Names for Scale Degrees.

Every scale degree has a technical name. Here are the names for each scale degree.

$\hat{1}$ Tonic
$\hat{2}$ Supertonic
$\hat{3}$ Mediant
$\hat{4}$ Subdominant
$\hat{5}$ Dominant
$\hat{6}$ Submediant
$\hat{7}$ Leading tone

1. 1. Write the following scales ascending and descending in whole notes Use a key signature for each.

G flat major

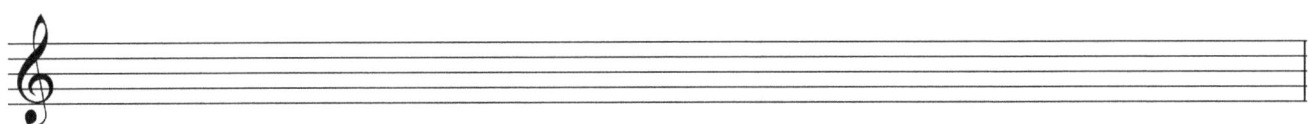

B major

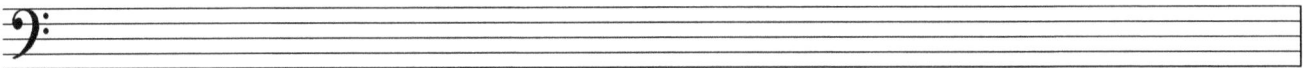

F sharp major

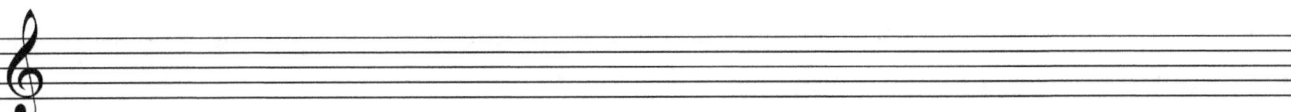

Minor Scale Review

There are three types of minor scales:

1. **natural minor**: uses the same key signature as its relative major.
2. **harmonic minor**: is the natural minor with $\hat{7}$ raised a half step.
3. **melodic minor**: is the natural minor with $\hat{6}$ and $\hat{7}$ raised a half step ascending, and lowered a half step descending.

Figure 1.3 show all three versions of the D minor scale.

Figure 1.3

D natural minor

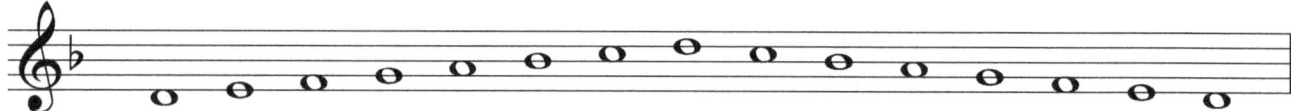

D harmonic minor

D melodic minor

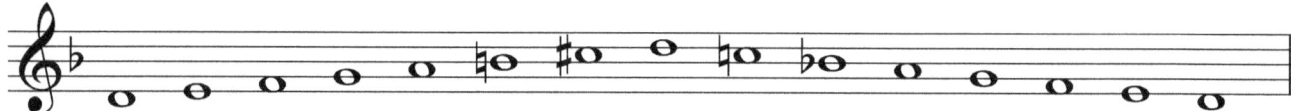

The Subtonic and the Leading Tone

There are two technical names for scale degree $\hat{7}$. The names depend on the scale and the relationship of $\hat{7}$ to the tonic.

When scale degree $\hat{7}$ occurs in the major scale it is one half step away from the tonic. In this case, it leads to the tonic and is called the **leading tone**.

When scale degree $\hat{7}$ is raised in the harmonic and ascending melodic minor scales it is one half step away from the tonic it is called the **leading tone**.

When scale degree $\hat{7}$ is not raised in the natural minor and the descending melodic minor scales, it is a whole step away from the tonic and is called the **subtonic**.

1. Write the following scales ascending and descending in whole notes. Use a key signature for each.

D flat major

The enharmonic tonic minor of D flat major, harmonic form

The relative minor of D flat major, melodic form

E flat minor, harmonic form

The parallel major of E flat minor

F sharp minor, natural form

The relative major of F sharp minor

C minor, melodic form

©San Marco Publications 2022   Scale Review

Finding The Key of a Composition

The key signature is the first level of organization in a piece of music. The key determines what pitches will occur in a piece. Key signatures are directly related to major and minor scales. A lot of the music we study today adheres to this system of major and minor, and knowing key signatures is an easy way to understand the key of a piece of music.

Study Figure 1.4. This melody has a key signature of three flats. This means that it is in the key of E♭ major or it's relative minor, C minor. The melody starts and ends on E♭ and does not contain any accidentals. Therefore it is in the key of E♭ major. It is important to note that this melody starts and ends on the tonic, but not all melodies will do this.

Figure 1.4

The melody in Figure 1.5 has a key signature of three flats indicating E♭ major or C minor. It also contains B♮. B♮ is not a note in the key of E♭ major. This is a clear indication of the key of C minor. B♮ is raised $\hat{7}$ of C minor. The melody also starts and ends on C, the tonic of C minor.

Figure 1.5

When determining the key of a melody consider the following:

1. The key signature and the two keys, major and minor, that it represents.
2. Accidentals. An accidental may be raised $\hat{7}$ or $\hat{6}$ of a minor key.
3. The beginning and ending notes. Melodies often start and end on the tonic of the key.
4. Look for chords that may be outlined in the melody. For example, a melody in G major may outline the G major triad G - B - D.

Sometimes the key of a melody will not be as clearly defined as the examples we have just seen. Study the melody in Figure 1.6. Two flats in the key signature indicate B♭ major or G minor. There are no accidentals in this melody. If it were in G minor, there should be raised $\hat{7}$ (F♯). However, this melody does not contain an F so we don't know if it would be raised. The first note is G, and the last note is G. The first measure outlines the notes of the G minor triad and the melody itself seems to center around the note G. In fact, G occurs five times. The key of this melody is G minor.

Figure 1.6

Minor key melodies may contain notes from the natural, harmonic, and melodic minor scales. The key signature of the melody in Figure 1.7 indicates F major or D minor. There are no accidentals. D minor may have raised $\hat{7}$ (C♯), but the one C in this melody is natural. The pick up is A followed by D on the first strong beat. The final note is D. The second measure outlines the notes of the D minor triad. The C♮ is in a descending line that indicates the melodic form of the D minor scale. A D minor melody may have B♭, B♮, C♯ or C♮ depending on how it is written, and the harmony it implies. This melody is in D minor.

Figure 1.7

Sometimes melodies contain accidentals that are used purely for chromatic decoration. These accidentals add color and variety to the music but are not part of the actual key. The melody in Figure 1.8 has the key signature of one sharp. This indicates G major or E minor. There is a C♯ in measure 2. In measure three, C is natural, and there are no D♯s anywhere in the melody. It starts and ends on G. Therefore, the C♯ is a chromatic decoration of the D on either side of it, or a more complex chord, and the melody is in the key of G major.

Figure 1.8

1. Name the keys of the following melodies.

2. Name the keys of the following musical excerpts.

Anton Diabelli
Allegretto

key:

Carl Czerny
Study

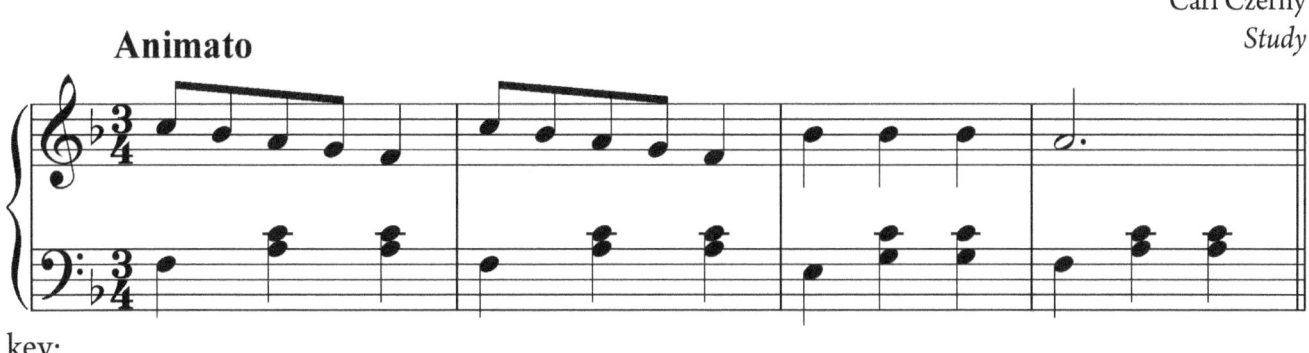

key:

Arcangelo Corelli
Sarabande

key:

Johannes Brahms
Waltz Op. 39. No. 3

key:

Finding a Key Without a Key Signature

You may have to determine the key of a composition that uses accidentals instead of a key signature. Follow these steps :

Determine if the melody uses flats or sharps. Figure 1.9 uses flats. List the flats in order and check them off as you find them in the music. This melody has two flats, B♭ and E♭. This indicates the keys of B♭ major or G minor. There are no other accidentals. G minor may have F♯, but F is not sharp here. The melody begins on B♭ and is in the key of B♭ major. It is written using a key signature in Figure 1.10.

Figure 1.9

Hector Berlioz
Symphony Fantastique, IV

B̶ E̶ A D G C F

Figure 1.10

Hector Berlioz
Symphony Fantastique, IV

The melody in Figure 1.11 uses sharps. Write the sharps in order and check them off as you find them in the music. There are three sharps. The keys of A major and F♯ minor have three sharps. However, there is no E♯ indicating raised $\hat{7}$ in F♯ minor. The music starts and ends on A. This is in the key of A major. This melody is written using a key signature in Figure 1.12.

Figure 1.11

Ludwig van Beethoven
Sonata no. 3 for Cello and Piano

F̶ C̶ G̶ D A E B

Figure 1.12

Ludwig van Beethoven
Sonata no. 3 for Cello and Piano

Figure 1.13 contains flats. However, B♭ is missing from the order of flats in this melody. You cannot have a key signature with E♭, A♭, and no B♭. We can assume that the B♮ is an accidental. This melody is in the key of C minor which has three flats and raised $\hat{7}$ (B♮). Figure 1.14 is the melody written using a key signature. B natural is needed for raised $\hat{7}$.

Figure 1.13

Antonio Vivaldi
Concerto

B ~~E~~ ~~A~~ D G C F

Figure 1.14

Antonio Vivaldi
Concerto

1. Name the keys of the following melodies. Rewrite them using a key signature and any necessary accidentals.

Joseph Haydn
Quartet, Op. 76

Key: _____

©San Marco Publications 2022

Scale Review

2

The Chromatic Scale

The *chromatic scale* is made up of half steps. It has twelve pitches. Since it contains the same intervals throughout it is considered a ***symmetric scale***. If you play a chromatic scale starting on C, you play every note ascending until you get to the next C, and then do the same descending. The notation of the chromatic scale may vary, but the simplest way to write a chromatic scale is to write sharps ascending and flats descending.

Figure 2.1 is an ascending chromatic scale starting on C. Sharps are used as the scale ascends. Half steps occur between E - F and B - C. When you write a chromatic scale, notate these white key half steps using natural notes. For example, don't write F as E♯.

Figure 2.1

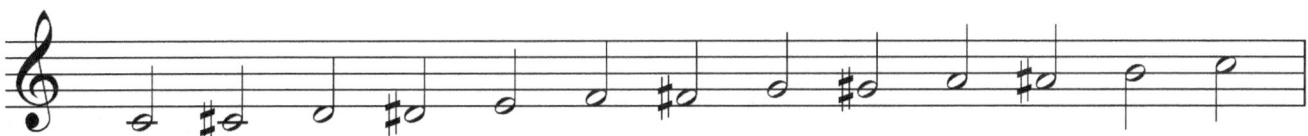

Figure 2.2 shows the C chromatic scale descending. Flats are used for the descending form of this scale. Flats are commonly used when notes move downward chromatically, and sharps are used for chromatic passages that ascend. The white key half steps C - B and F - E are notated as natural notes.

Figure 2.2

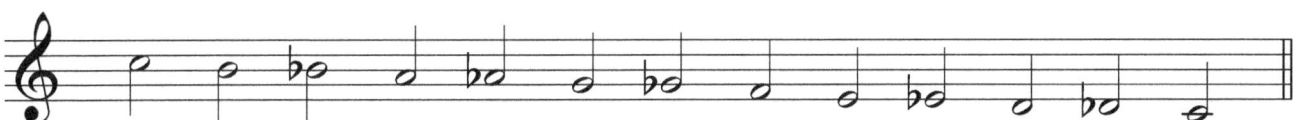

When writing the chromatic scale ascending and descending and it is a good idea to use a bar line at the top of the scale before moving down. This cancels all the previous accidentals. See Figure 2.3.

- When writing any chromatic scale do not use the same letter name more than twice.
- Never change the name of the tonic enharmonically. For example, if the scale starts on C♯ it must end on C♯, not on D♭.

Figure 2.3

When a chromatic scale starts on a flat, use sharps as soon as possible as you ascend. The A♭ chromatic scale in Figure 2.4 cannot change to sharps until C♯ because no letter name can be used more than twice. Notice that it does not end on G♯ at the top. It must end on the same note that it starts, in this case, A♭.

Figure 2.4

1. Write the following chromatic scales ascending and descending.

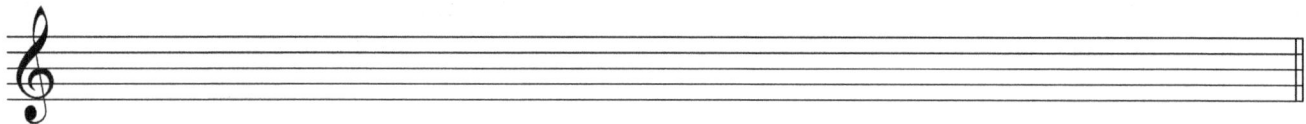

Chromatic scale on F

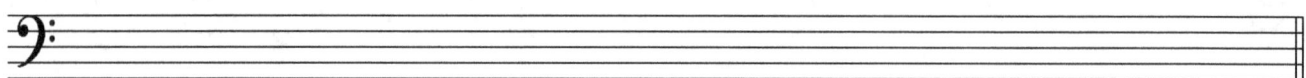

Chromatic scale on D♭

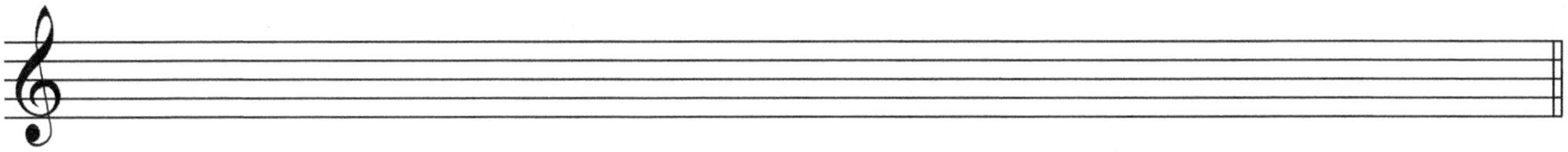

Chromatic scale on E

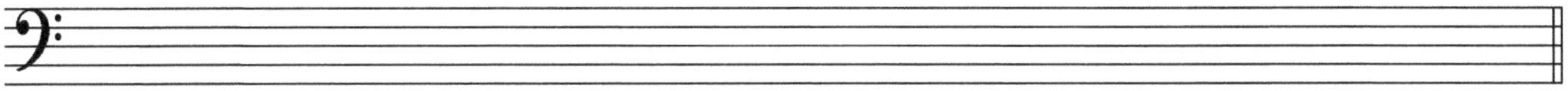

Chromatic scale on G#

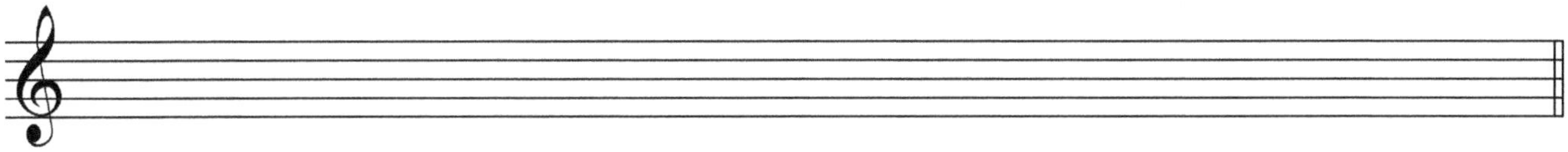

Chromatic scale on A

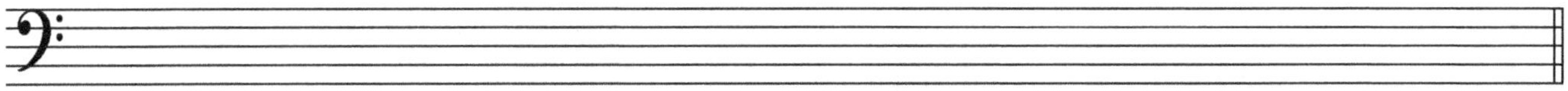

Chromatic scale on G♭

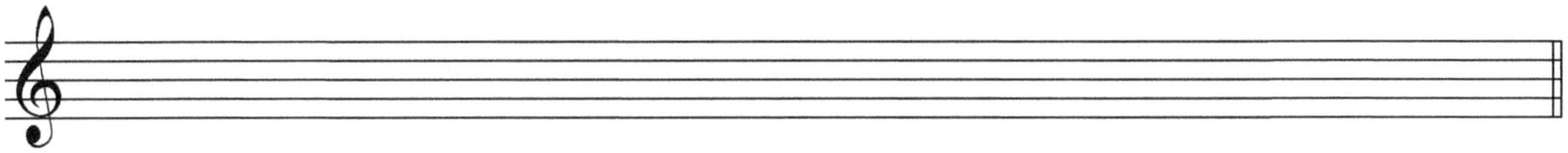

Chromatic scale on B

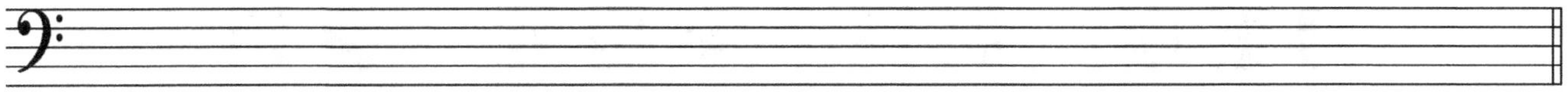

Chromatic scale on F#

The notation of a chromatic scale may vary if it is written in a specific key. In this case, the key signature will be the guide to the accidentals used in the chromatic scale.

For example, if a sharp-based key signature is used, sharps are used for the chromatic notes in the scale. The D chromatic scale in Figure 2.5 uses the key signature of D major. Since this is a key signature using sharps, the chromatic scale uses sharps. It is important to be aware of the key signature and adjust any notes accordingly.

Figure 2.5

The chromatic scale in the key of B♭ uses the key signature of B♭ major. This is a flat-based key signature. The added chromatic scale notes are not part of that key. However, since the key signature uses flats, the chromatic scale uses flats ascending and descending.

Figure 2.6 is the B♭ flat chromatic scale using a key signature. When writing this scale, begin with the key signature and the starting note. Since flats are used in the key of B♭ major, move each note up and down chromatically using flats. It is helpful to think of the keyboard when writing chromatic scales. Never use a letter name more than twice.

Figure 2.6

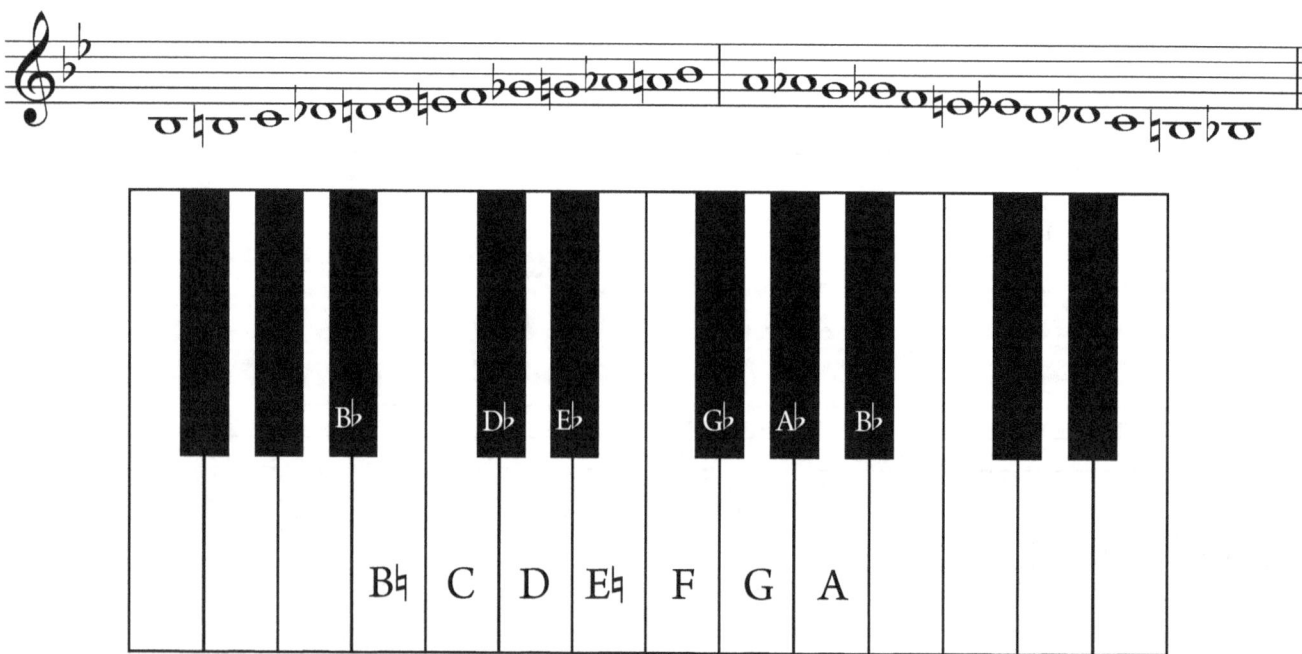

1. Write the following chromatic scales using key signatures for each.

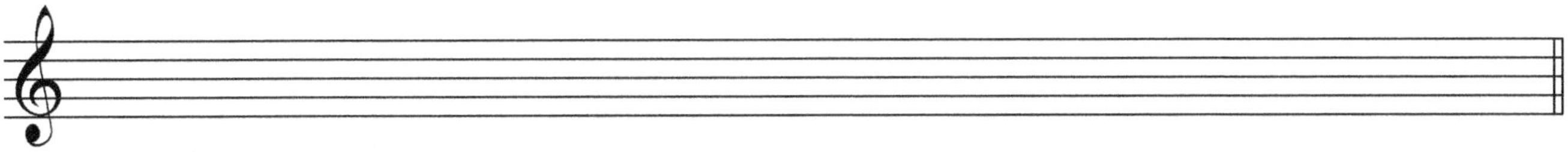

F chromatic scale

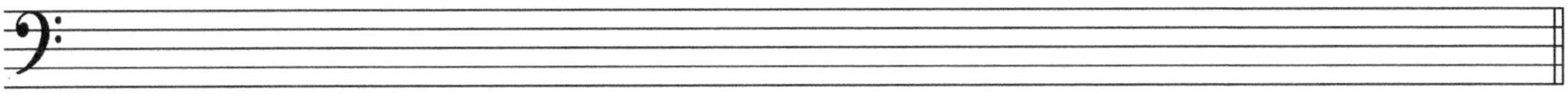

A chromatic scale

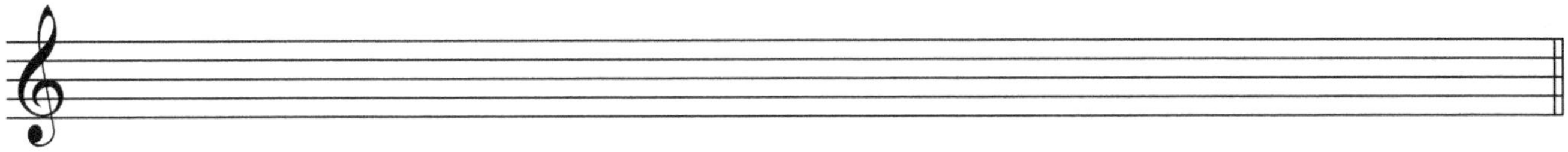

E♭ chromatic scale

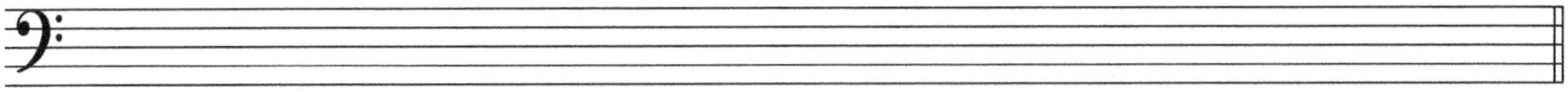

B chromatic scale

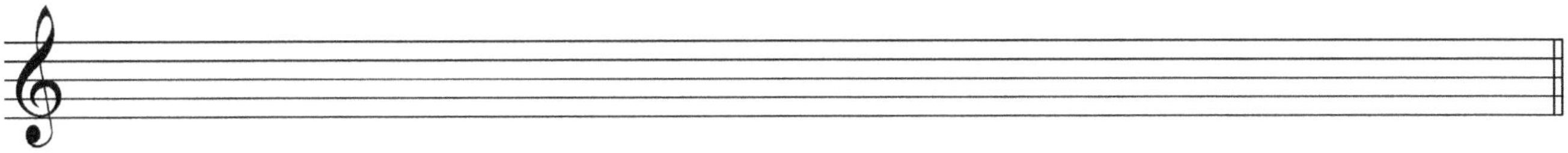

A♭ chromatic scale

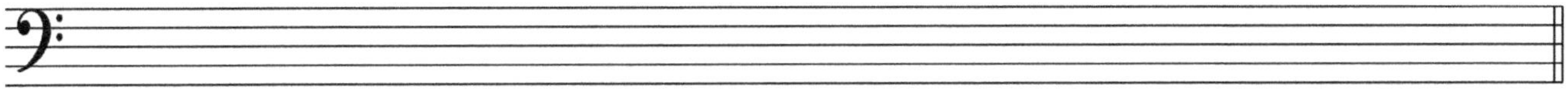

F♯ chromatic scale

2. Circle any chromatic passages that occur in the following musical excerpts.

Henry Purcell
Dido and Aeneas, Didos Lament

Ludwig van Beethoven
Sonata Op. 2, No. 2, IV

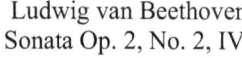

The Chromatic Scale

3
The Whole Tone Scale

The *whole tone scale* is a symmetric scale. It is constructed entirely of whole steps. This is a six-note scale. There are two different whole tone scales. One starting on C, and one starting on C♯. Starting on any other note will create the same pitches as those starting on C or C♯.

Figure 3.1 shows these whole tone scales. When writing this scale:

- Start and end on the same note. Do not change the tonic enharmonically.
- Use six different letter names.
- Do not mix sharps and flats. Use one or the other.

The whole tone scale is often used in movie music during dream sequences since it has a unique dreamy sound. Composers in the twentieth century, most notably Claude Debussy, used this scale in their compositions.

Figure 3.1

1. Add accidentals to the following to create whole tone scales.

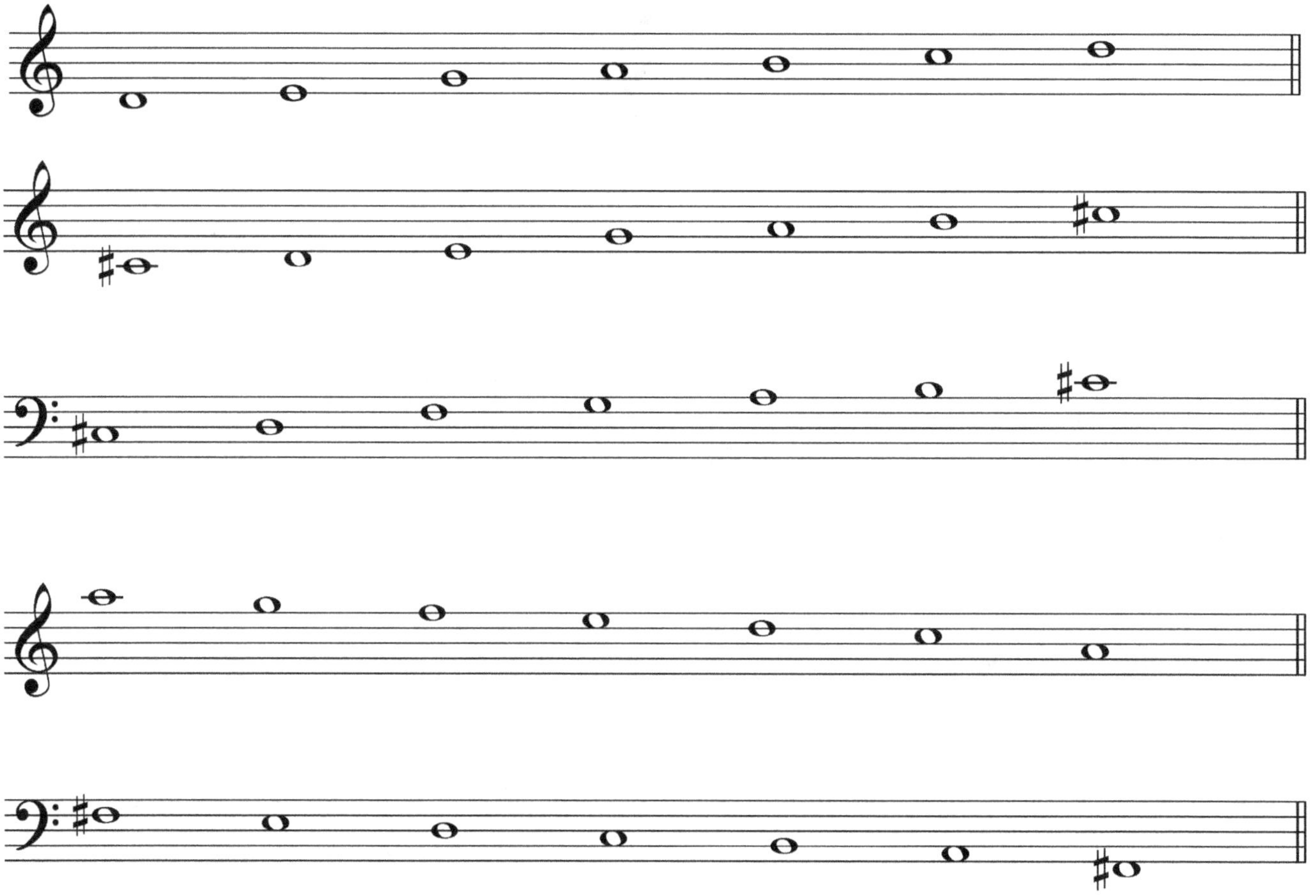

2. Write whole tone scales ascending and descending on the following notes.

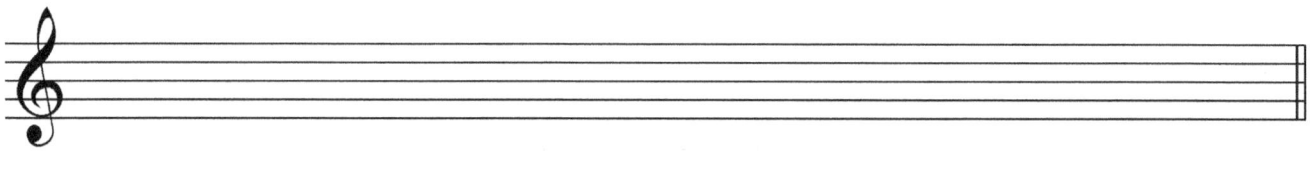

on G♭

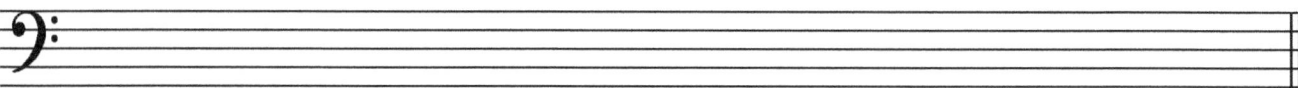

on B

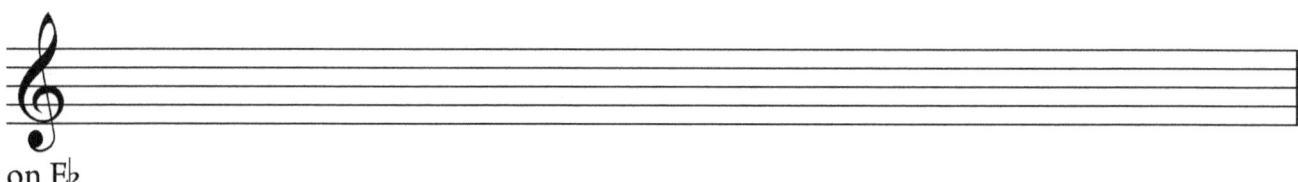

on E♭

Whole Tone Scale

4

The Octatonic Scale

The *octatonic* or *diminished scale*, as it is sometimes known, has eight different notes ("octa" means eight). The octatonic scale is a symmetrical scale. It is built using alternating whole and half steps. There are two forms of this scale. One starts with a whole step followed by a half step. The other starts with a half step followed by a whole step.

Figure 4.1 shows the two versions of this scale starting on C. Composers, like Stravinsky, Scriabin, and Bartok used this scale. It is common in jazz music as well.

Figure 4.1

Whole - Half Octatonic

Half - Whole Octatonic

There are only three octatonic scales. The octatonic scales built on C, C♯, and D are the only ones that use unique sets of notes. If you start an octatonic scale on any other note you will get scales with notes identical to those found on C, C♯, or D.

It is important not to change the first note of this scale enharmonically. For example, if it starts on C♯, it must end on C♯.

1. Add accidentals to create octatonic scales. Do not change the first note of each scale.

2. Write the following octatonic scales ascending and descending.

E octatonic, starting with a whole step

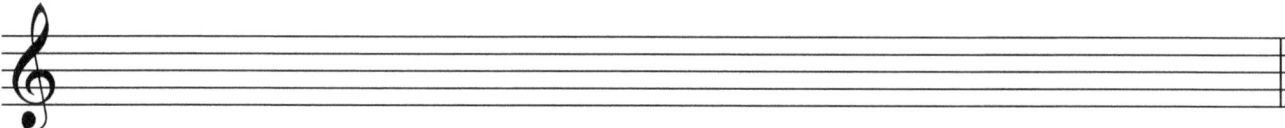

C♯ octatonic, starting with a half step

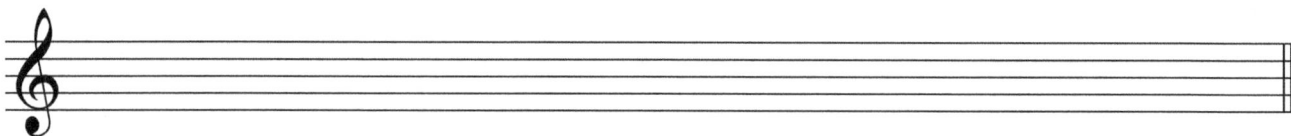

A♭ octatonic, starting with a whole step

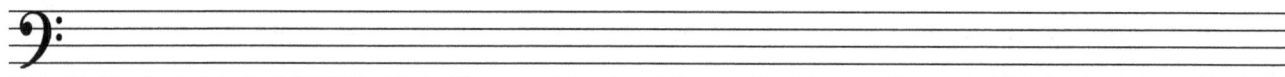

G octatonic, starting with a half step

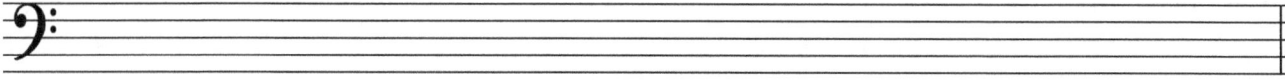

5
Pentatonic Scales

Pentatonic scales are five note scales. The prefix "penta" is from the Greek meaning five, and tonic means tones or notes. Pentatonic scales are used in folk, rock, jazz and church music. There are two types of pentatonic scales: major and minor.

The Major Pentatonic Scale

The **major pentatonic scale** is a five-note scale that is related to the major scale. In the major pentatonic scale two notes are omitted from the major scale: $\hat{4}$ and $\hat{7}$.

The C major pentatonic scale is: C D E G A C. This is shown in Figure 5.1.

Figure 5.1

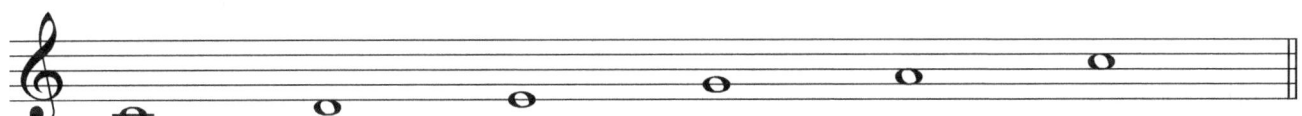

1. Write the following major pentatonic scales ascending only.

D major pentatonic

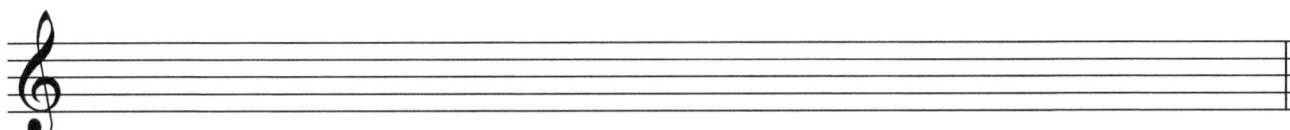

F major pentatonic

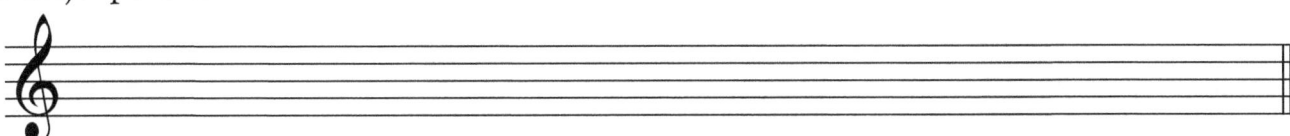

E♭ major pentatonic

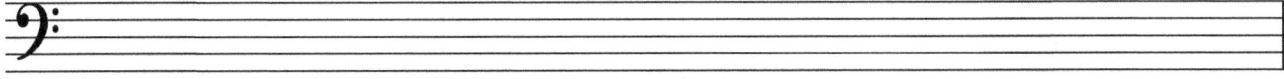

The Minor Pentatonic Scale

The *minor pentatonic scale* is another five note scale. This scale is a natural minor scale with two notes removed. To form a minor pentatonic scale, remove $\hat{2}$ and $\hat{6}$ from the natural minor scale. The A minor pentatonic scale is: A C D E G A. This scale is shown in Figure 5.2.

Figure 5.2

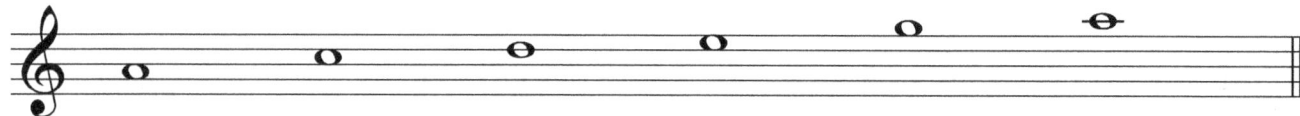

1. Write the following minor pentatonic scales ascending only.

G minor pentatonic

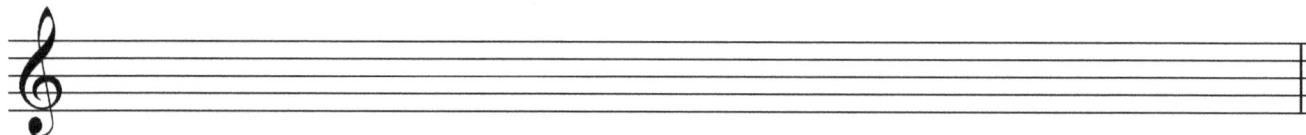

E minor pentatonic

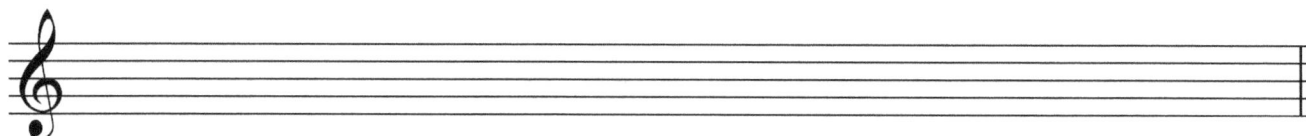

C minor pentatonic

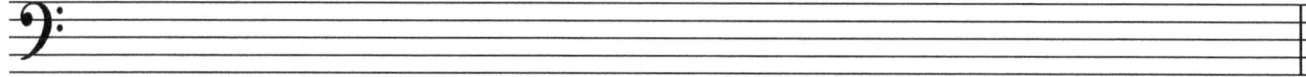

B minor pentatonic

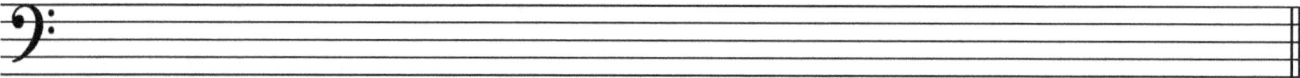

6

The Blues Scale

The *blues scale* can be created by altering notes of the major scale. The altered notes are called "blue" notes. These notes originated with African slaves brought to America. A blue note was created by bending the pitch of a note when singing.

The blues scale is the major scale with $\hat{3}$, $\hat{5}$ and $\hat{7}$ lowered a half step. $\hat{5}$ occurs twice, once lowered and once in its original form. Scale degrees $\hat{2}$ and $\hat{6}$ are omitted.

Figure 6.1 contains the C blues scale.

Figure 6.1

1. Add accidentals to the following to create blues scales.

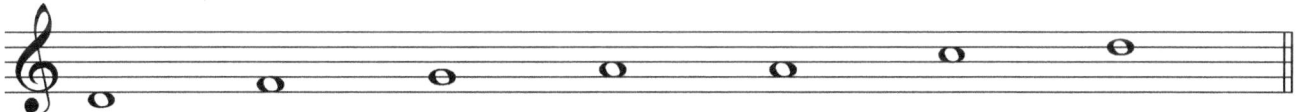

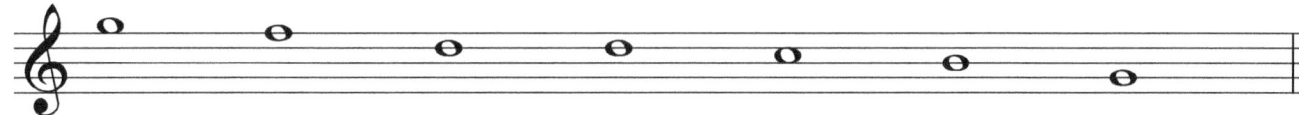

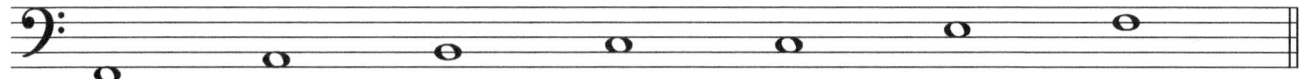

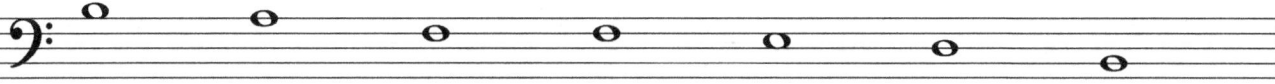

2. Write the following blues scales ascending.

E blues

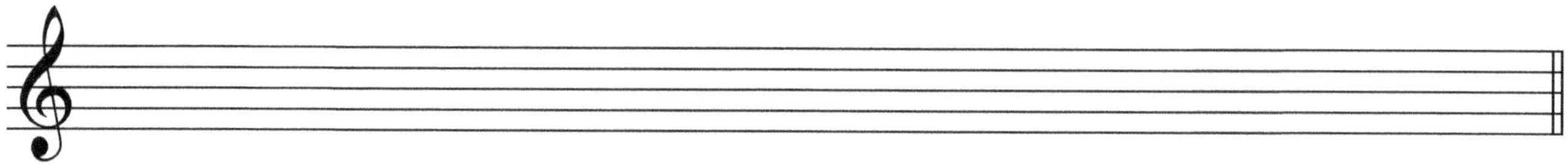

A♭ blues

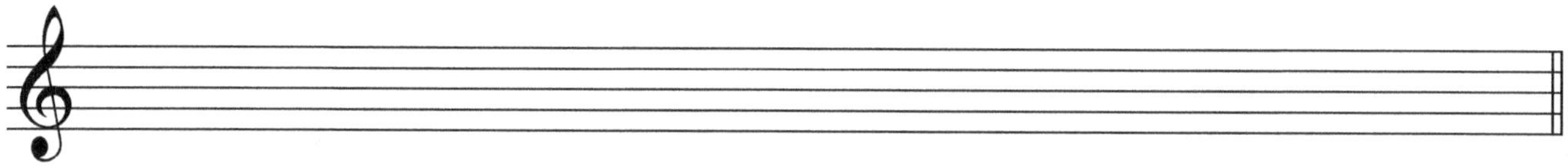

G blues

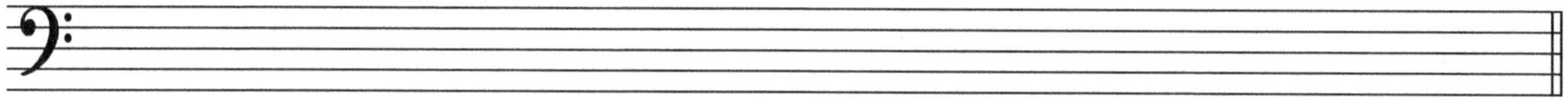

F blues

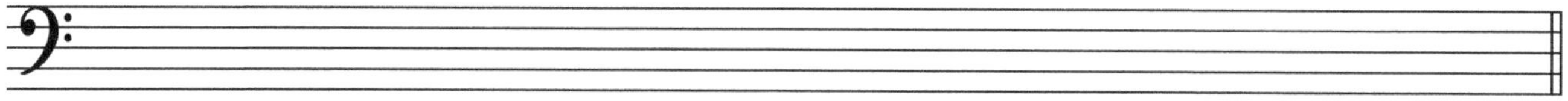

3. Write the following blues scales descending.

A blues

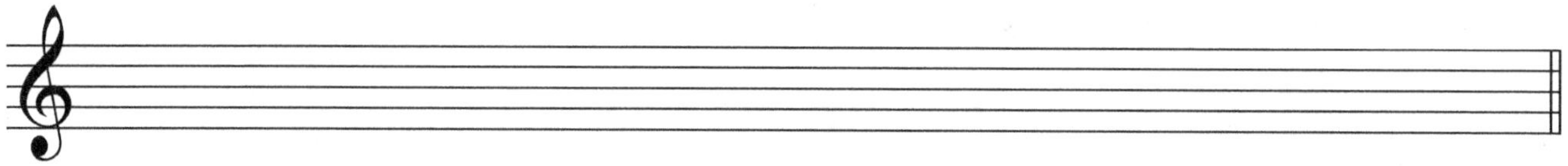

C blues

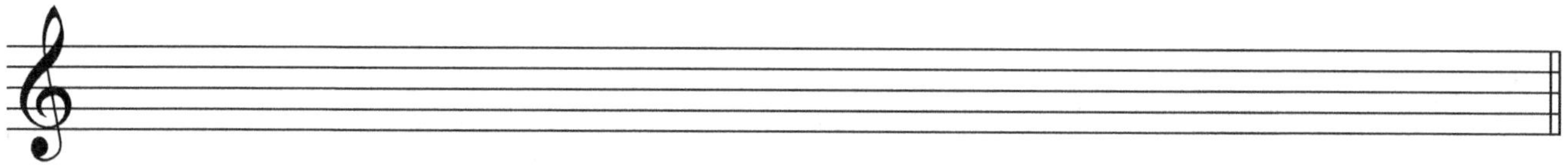

B blues

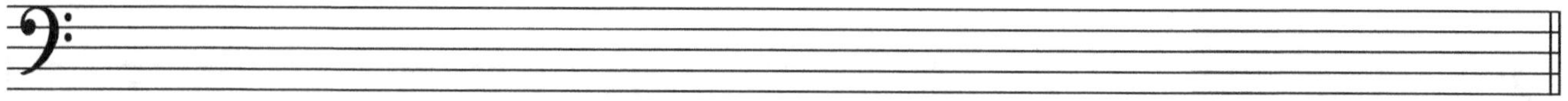

D blues

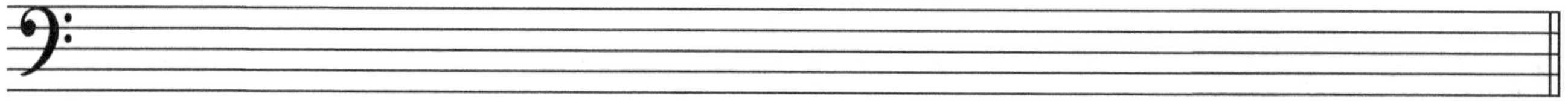

4. Identify the following scales as: major, natural minor, harmonic minor, melodic minor, chromatic, whole tone, octatonic, major pentatonic, minor pentatonic, or blues.

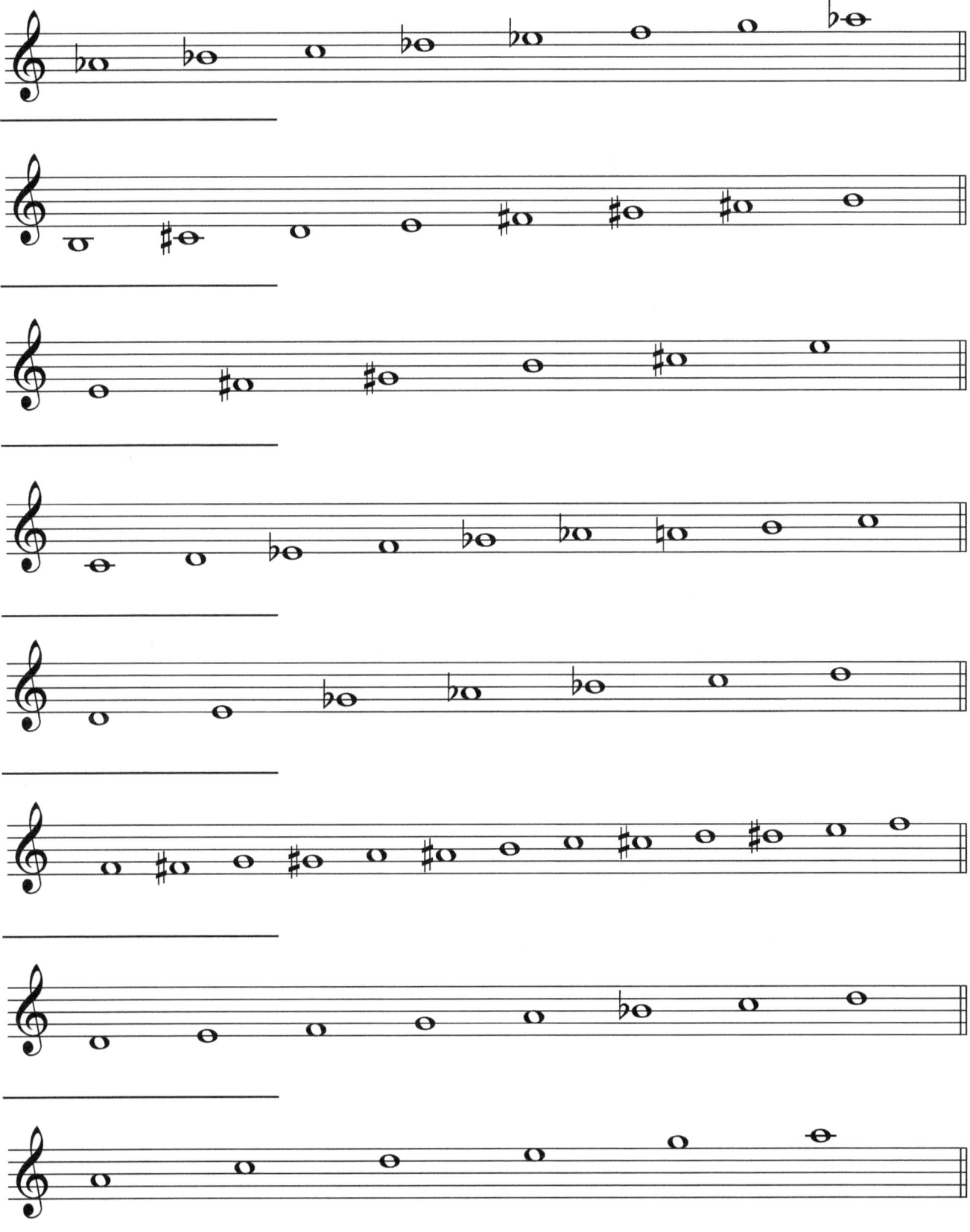

7
History 1

The Romantic Era (ca 1825 - 1900)

The **Romantic era** comes after the Classical era. This period covers most of the 19th century, from about the years 1825 to 1900.

Romanticism was a cultural movement that started in Europe. This movement influenced philosophical thinking, literature, music, and art.

Romantic music was influenced by the literature and painting of the era. It was marked with deep emotional expression. Romantic music expressed strong feelings through music. It was more pictorial than earlier music and often attempted to describe something, perhaps a scene in nature, a poem, a story, or a particular feeling. Music that has a literary or pictorial association is called **program music**. Pieces were often given descriptive titles like Album Leaf, Nocturne, Impromptu, Humoresque, Intermezzo, Arabesque, Papillons.

A few of the composers from this period include Franz Schubert, Frédéric Chopin, Franz Liszt, Robert Schumann, Johannes Brahms, Felix Mendelssohn, Edvard Grieg, Piotr Ilyich Tchaikovsky, Guisseppe Verdi, Georges Bizet, and many more.

Felix Mendelssohn (1809 - 1847)

Felix Mendelssohn was born in 1809 in Hamburg, Germany to a wealthy family with parents who encouraged him to be a musician.

Mendelssohn was the most celebrated child prodigy since Mozart. He began taking piano lessons from his mother when he was 6 and made his first public concert appearance at the age of 9. As a child, he composed extensively, writing five short operas and 11 symphonies by the time he was in his teens.

Mendelssohn came from a musical family. His sister Fanny was also an excellent pianist and composer. The two of them put on Shakespeare's comedy A Midsummer Night's Dream to entertain family and friends and played all of the characters. Mendelssohn's music for A Midsummer Night's Dream describes the plot and many characters in the play.

Mendelssohn's grandfather was the Jewish philosopher Moses Mendelssohn. Being Jewish in Germany was difficult for the Mendelssohn family. They lived at a time when there were specific taxes and laws that only applied to Jews. Because of this discrimination against Jewish people, (known as anti-Semitism), Mendelssohn's father decided to convert to Christianity and changed the family name to Mendelssohn-Bartholdy.

Mendelssohn can be given credit for reviving the music of Johann Sebastian Bach which was largely forgotten by the 19th century. In 1829 he conducted a performance of Bach's St. Matthew Passion, a work for orchestra, choir and soloists. The concert was so successful it started a renewed and lasting appreciation for the music of Bach.

Mendelssohn traveled extensively. His trips to other countries inspired some of his best music. The Italian and Scottish symphonies were inspired by his travels and are two examples of *exoticism*. Exoticism is a term used to describe music that evokes the atmosphere of far-off lands or cultures. Mendelssohn, a German, wrote symphonies inspired by lands that were not part of his heritage.

Mendelssohn died in 1847 at the age of 38 after suffering from ill health. His life was short. However, he managed to distinguish himself as one of the greatest composers of the Romantic period.

Overture to a Midsummer Nights Dream

A German translation of the Shakespeare play " A Midsummer Nights Dream" became part of the Mendelssohn's library in 1826. Felix loved it and wrote this overture in 1827 when he was just 17 years old.

The genre of this composition is *concert overture*. A concert overture is a single movement concert piece for symphony orchestra based on a literary idea. Overture to a Midsummer Nights Dream is written for two flutes, two oboes, two clarinets, two bassoons, two horns, two trumpets, ophicleide, timpani, and strings. An ophicleide is a bass brass instrument with keys that was eventually replaced by the tuba.

A concert overture is considered *program music*. Program music is music that has a literary or pictorial association. It has an extra-musical meaning and evokes images or ideas.

A Midsummer Nights Dream is based on the Shakespeare play of the same name. It involves fairies, love potions, and some very bizarre ideas. The play ends by telling the audience it was nothing but a dream.

A concert overture is a romantic piece, but Mendelssohn uses a few classical elements like sonata form. Sonata form consists of three sections:

1. **The Exposition.** In this section, the composer introduces themes that will be used throughout the composition. There are usually two contrasting themes, and this section ends in a new key (the dominant or relative major).

2. **The Development.** In this section, the composer develops the themes from the exposition. This may be done by exploring motives and sequences based on the themes, but the main feature of the development is the exploration of different keys.

3. **The Recapitulation.** Here, the themes from the exposition return in the tonic key. This section remains in the tonic key and often ends with a *coda*. Coda means "tail" in Italian. A coda is a concluding section of a piece of music. Its length can vary, but it adds a final embellishment to the end of a composition.

Mendelssohn's overture is in the key of E major, and it begins with an introduction before the exposition starts. This consists of four magical chords that give you the impression that you are in a dream (Figure 7.1). These chords are played by the wind instruments. They invite the listener to a magical forest near Athens where the play is set.

Figure 7.1

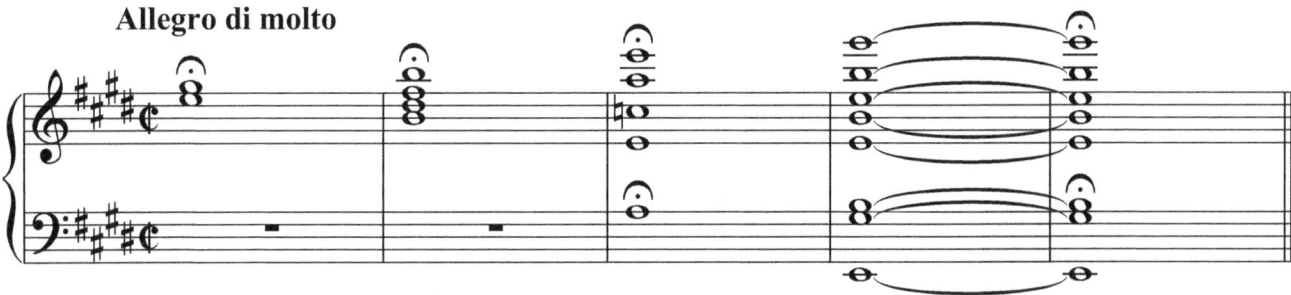

Figure 7.2 contains the first theme in the exposition. This theme is played by the violins and depicts the fairies scurrying through the woods. It is written in the tonic minor, E minor.

Figure 7.2

A fanfare-like transition leads to the second theme. The first part shown in Figure 7.3 is played by the full orchestra and portrays the lovers. The second part shown in Figure 7.4 paints a musical picture of the character named Bottom after Puck's magic has turned him into a donkey. His "hee-hawing" is played by the strings.

Figure 7.3

Figure 7.4

The exposition is followed by the development section and the recapitulation. The overture ends with the same four magical chords with which it started. Mendelssohn starts the piece like a dream and completes it in the same way, interpreting Shakespeare's play perfectly.

Music Terms

Study the following Italian terms and their meanings.

agitato	agitated
dolente	sad
giocoso	humorous, joyful
grandioso	grand, play in a grand and noble style
martellato	strongly accented, hammered
morendo	dying, fading away
mesto	sad, mournful
pesante	heavy, play with weight
risoluto	resolute, bold, strong
scherzando	playful, play in a light-hearted happy manner
sostentuto	sustained, play in a prolonged manner
vivo	lively

Review 1

1. Write the following scales ascending and descending using key signatures where applicable.

G♭ major

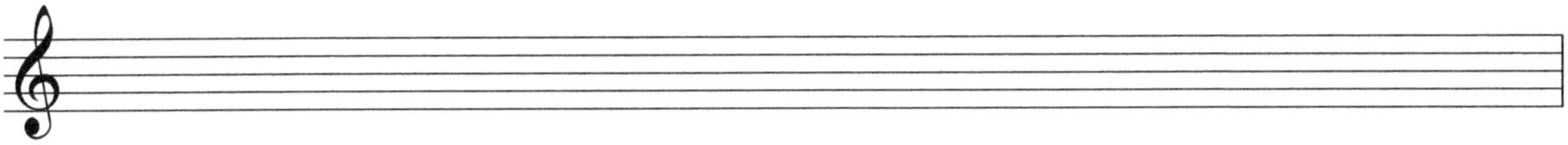

G♭ major's enharmonic tonic minor, harmonic form

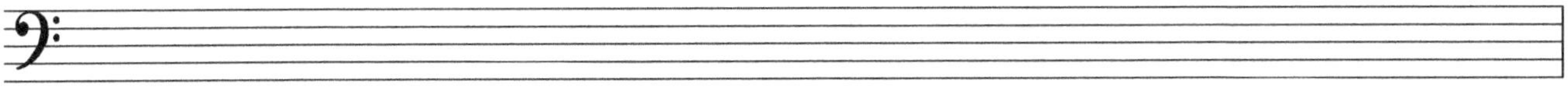

E chromatic

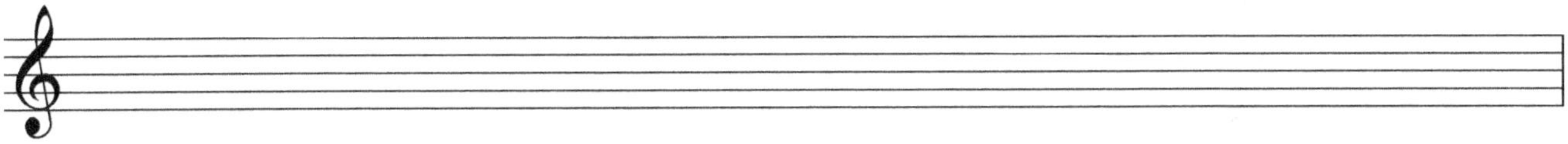

B♭ whole tone

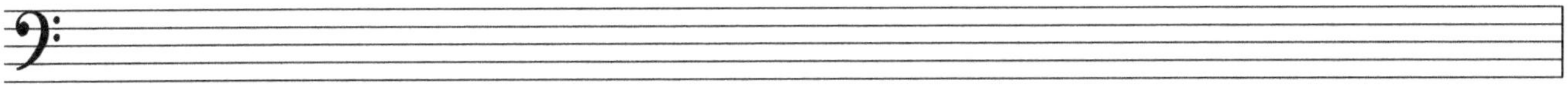

A octatonic

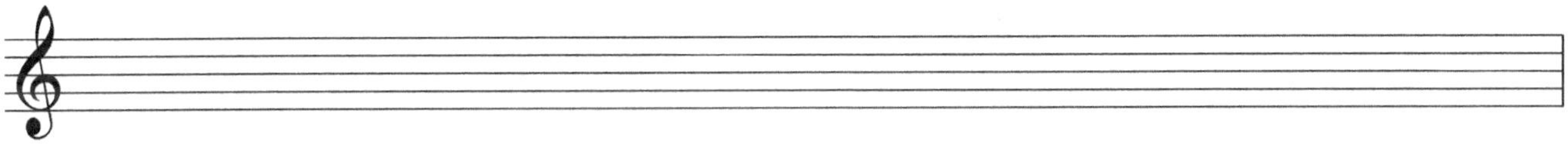

F♯ major pentatonic

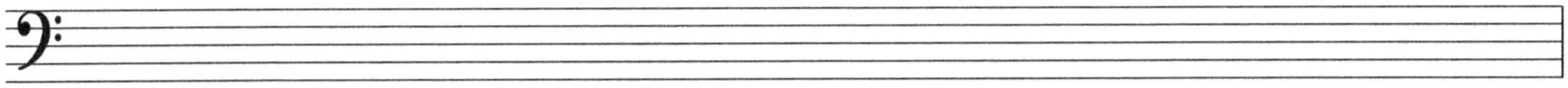

D minor pentatonic

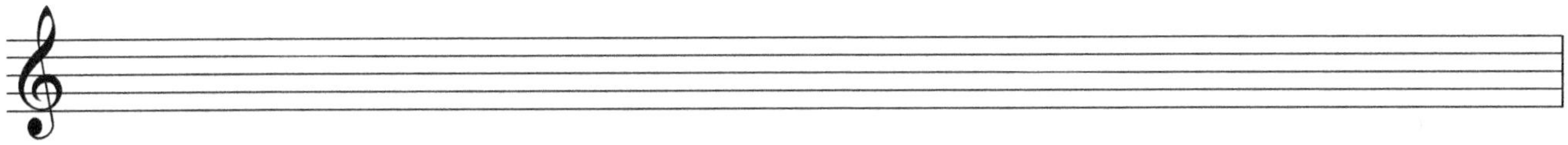

G blues

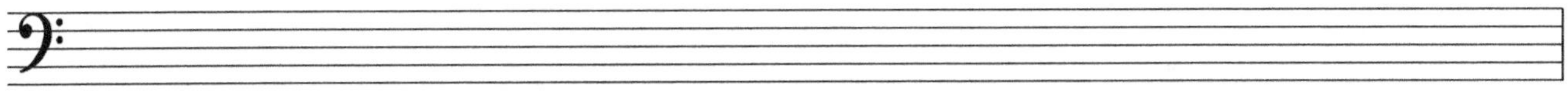

2. When did the Romantic era occur? _____

3. Music that has a literary or pictorial association is called _____

4. Name two Romantic period composers _____

5. Where was Felix Mendelssohn born? _____

6. Whose music did Mendelssohn help revive? _____

7. What genre is Overture to a Midsummer Nights Dream? _____

8. What author wrote the play that this work is based upon? _____

9. What is the form of Overture to a Midsummer Nights Dream? _____

10. Name the three main sections in this form:

_____ _____ _____

11. Match the Italian terms with their meanings.

agitato _____   a) lively

dolente _____   b) grand, play in a grand and noble style

giocoso _____   c) resolute, bold, strong

grandioso _____   d) sad

mesto _____   e) sustained, play in a prolonged manner

risoluto _____   f) humorous, joyful

sostentuto _____   g) sad, mournful

vivo _____   h) agitated

8
Intervals

Review

The interval is a unit of measurement in music. It represents the distance between two pitches. Study the intervals in Figure 8.1. In order for an interval to be major or perfect the top note must be a member of the bottom notes scale.

In a), B is the third note of the G major scale, making it a major 3rd. If the top note is lowered one half step, (B♭) it becomes minor. If the top note is lowered a whole step, (B♭♭) it becomes diminished.

In b), when the bottom note is raised one half step (G♯) it becomes minor. When the bottom note is raised a whole step it becomes diminished.

In c) and d), the major interval becomes augmented by raising the top note one half step (B♯) or lowering the bottom note one half step (G♭).

Perfect intervals (1, 4, 5, 8) never become minor. In e), lowering the top one half step makes the 4th diminished. Raising the top note a half step makes it augmented.

Figure 8.1

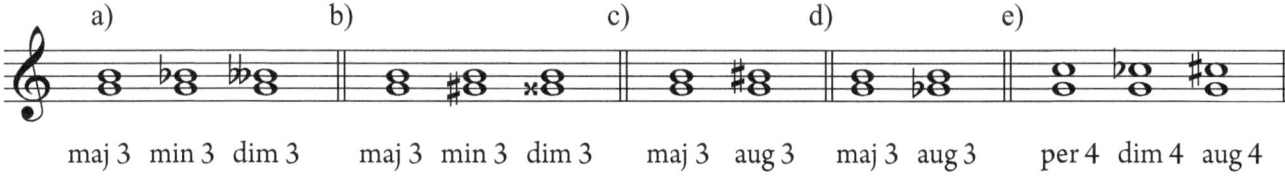

The unison requires special consideration. Since there is no distance between the notes of a unison, it cannot be made smaller. Unisons can never be diminished intervals. If any note of a unison is altered, the notes become further away from each other, and it becomes augmented. Study Figure 8.2.

Figure 8.2

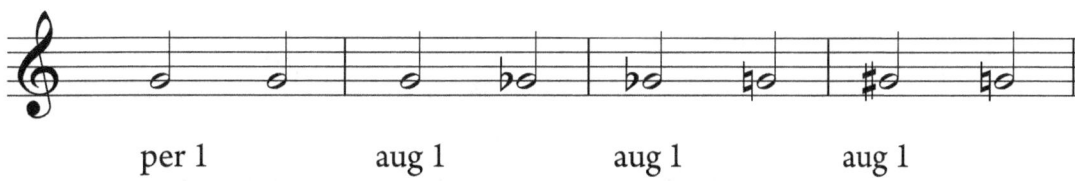

This chart shows the relationship between intervals. The arrow indicates the movement of the top note one half step.

diminished ← minor ← **major** → augmented

diminshed ← **perfect** → augmented

Solving Intervals

Use the following steps to determine an interval:

1. Count the notes from the bottom up to determine the interval number. Always start by counting the bottom note as 1. In Figure 8.3 A to F is a 6th. A-B-C-D-E-F is 1-2-3-4-5-6.
2. Determine, by the number, if the interval should be major or perfect. A 6th would be major interval.
3. Decide if the top note is a member of the bottom notes major scale. Here, F♮ is not a member of the A major scale since A major has an F♯. It has been lowered one half step making this interval a minor 6th.

Intervals are always solved using the lowest note as the key note. This is true even if the lowest note comes after the highest note in a melodic interval. The lowest note in the second interval in Figure 8.3 comes after the highest note but the interval is still a minor 6th.

Figure 8.3

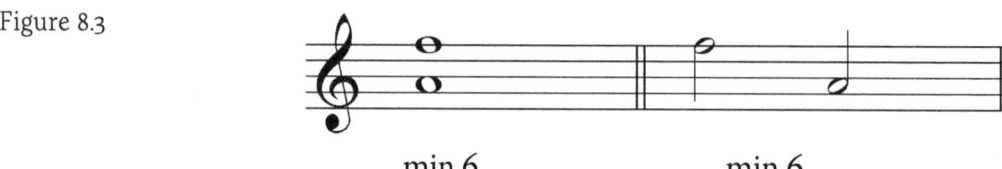

min 6   min 6

1. Name the following intervals.

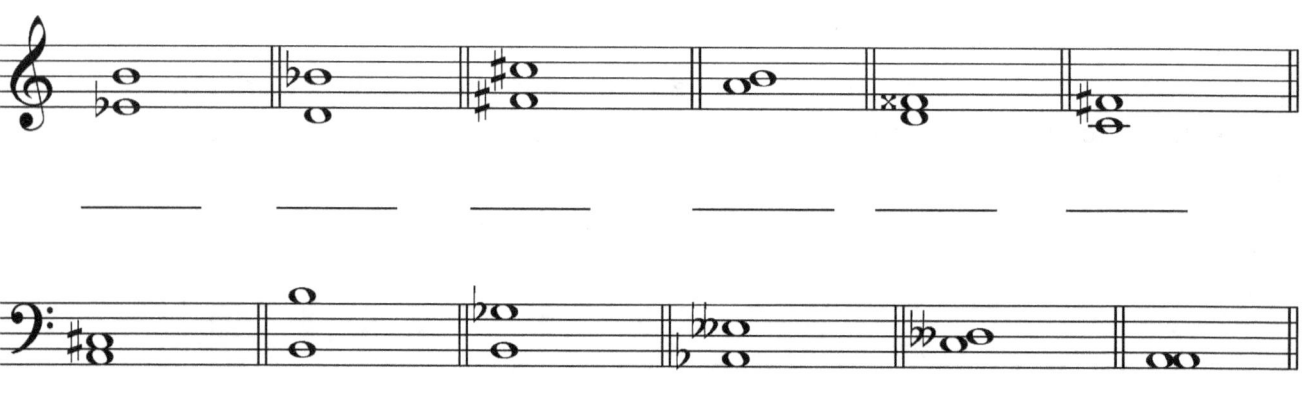

Writing an Interval Below a Given Note

You may be asked to write an interval below a given note. Let's say you have to write a major 6th below C. Figure 8.4. illustrates the following steps.

1. Write the note that is a 6th below C.
2. A 6th below C is E.
3. Check the interval quality. In this case E to C is a minor 6th. We need a major 6th, so you have to lower the E to E♭ in order to get a major 6th. Note: You cannot change the given note (C).

Figure 8.4

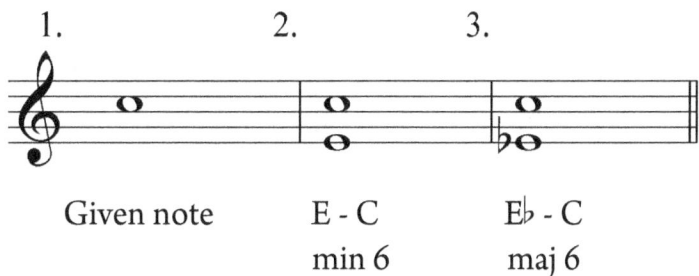

1. Write the following intervals below the given notes.

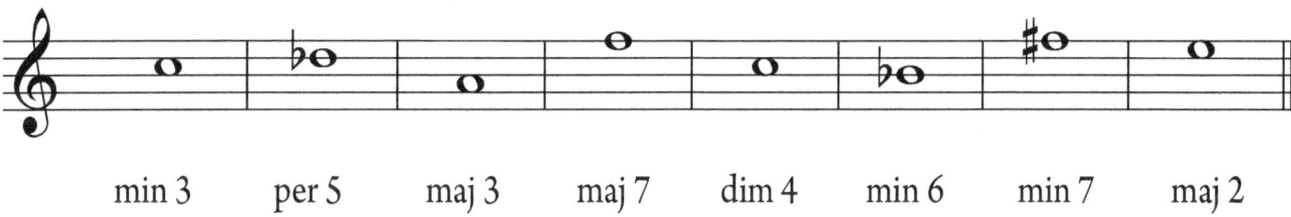

min 3   per 5   maj 3   maj 7   dim 4   min 6   min 7   maj 2

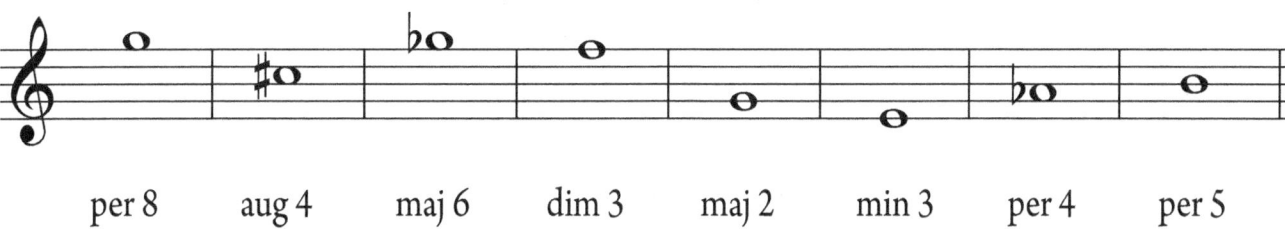

per 8   aug 4   maj 6   dim 3   maj 2   min 3   per 4   per 5

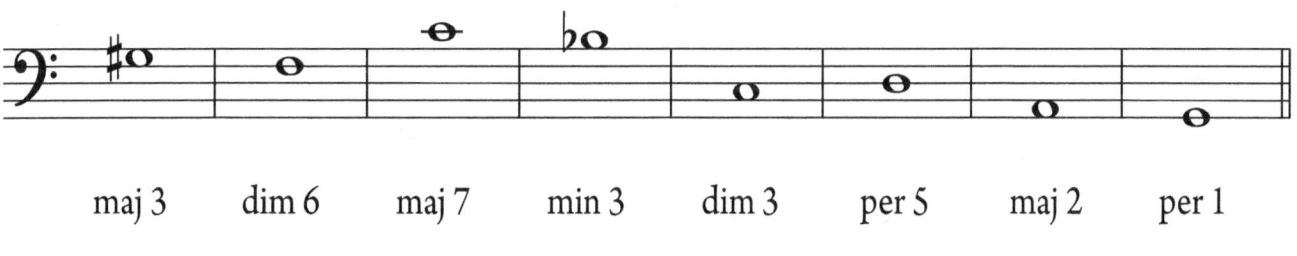

maj 3   dim 6   maj 7   min 3   dim 3   per 5   maj 2   per 1

Inverting Intervals

Any interval can be inverted or flipped upside down. Figure 8.5 shows the perfect 4th G - C inverted in the second measure. When you invert a perfect 4th it becomes a perfect 5th. Here, C -G.

Figure 8.5

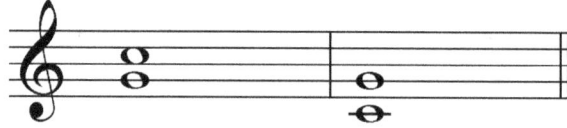

When an interval is inverted the sum of the original and the inverted interval equals nine. Using the intervals in Figure 8.5, G -C is a perfect 4th. When it is inverted it becomes C-G, a perfect 5th. When you add 4 and 5 you get 9. Study the interval inversions in Figure 8.6. They all add up to 9.

Figure 8.6

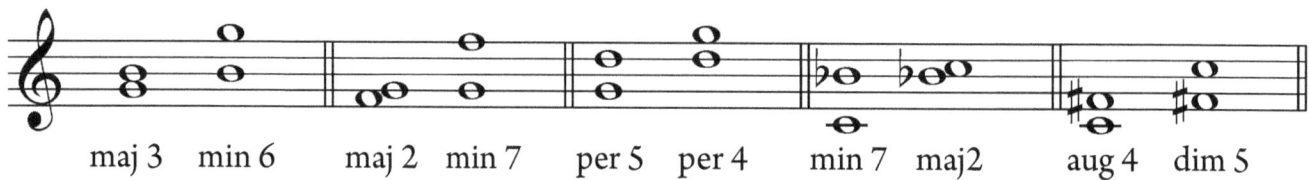

Except for perfect intervals the interval quality changes when you invert them. Here is what happens to the interval qualities when you invert them:

- major becomes minor
- minor becomes major
- diminished becomes augmented
- augmented becomes diminshed
- perfect stays perfect

The augmented octave is a special case when inverting. An augmented octave is larger than an octave and when it is inverted the numbers do not add up to 9. Figure 8.7 shows the inversion of the augmented octave. An aug 8 becomes a dim 8 when inverted. However, since a dim 8 is smaller than an octave, it becomes and aug 1 when inverted.

Figure 8.7

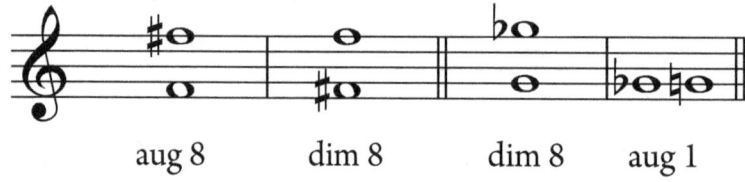

1. Name the following intervals. In the staff below, invert them and rename them.

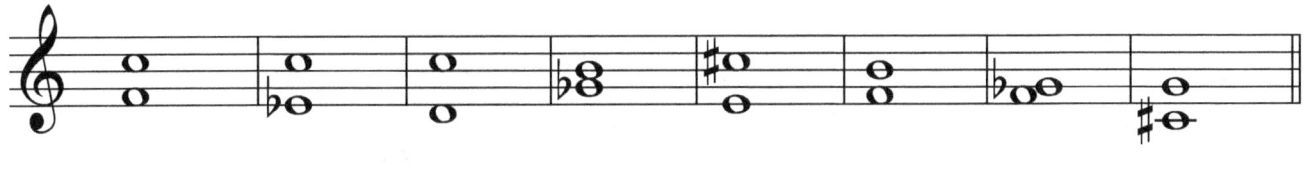

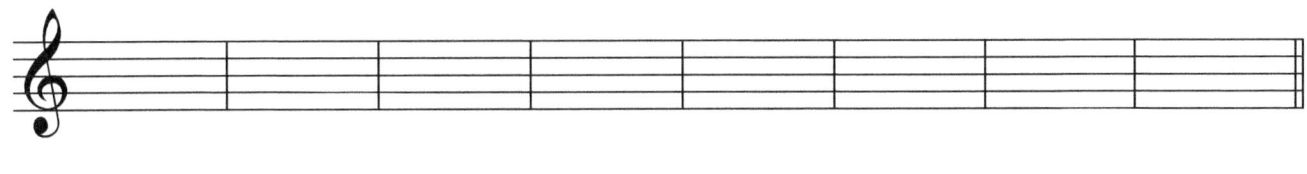

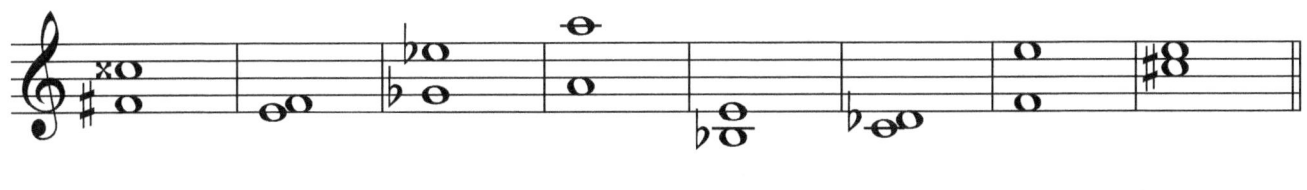

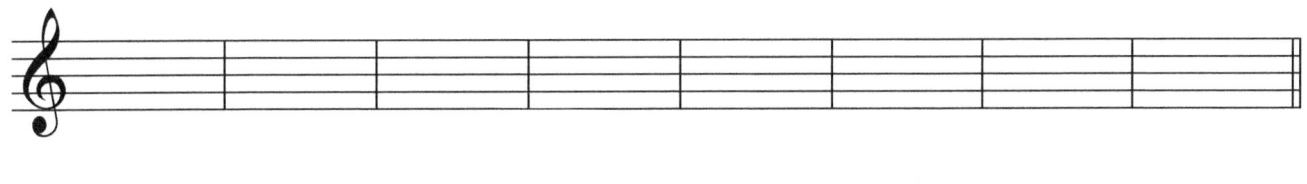

2. Name the following intervals.

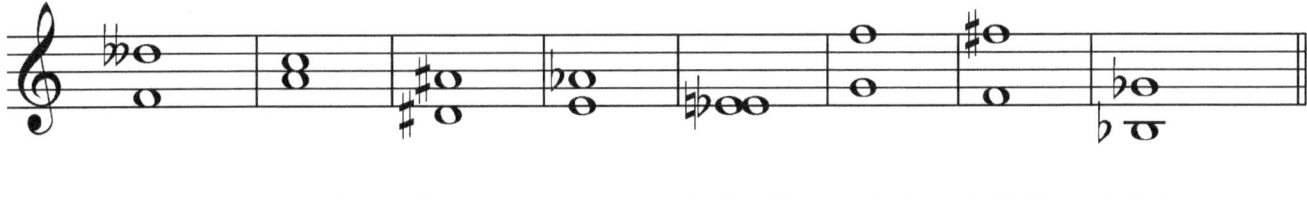

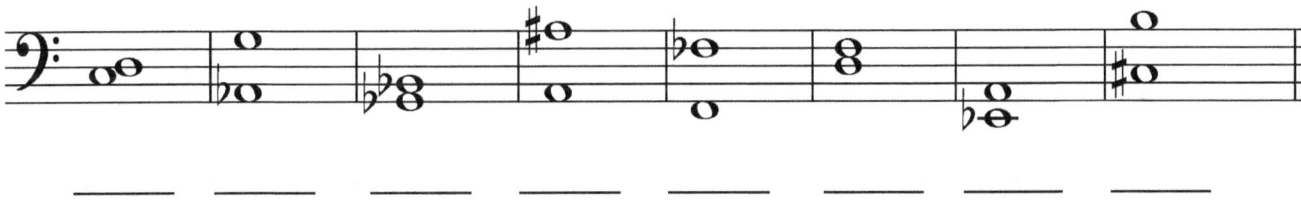

Intervals

3. Write the following intervals above the given notes. Invert them and name the inversions.

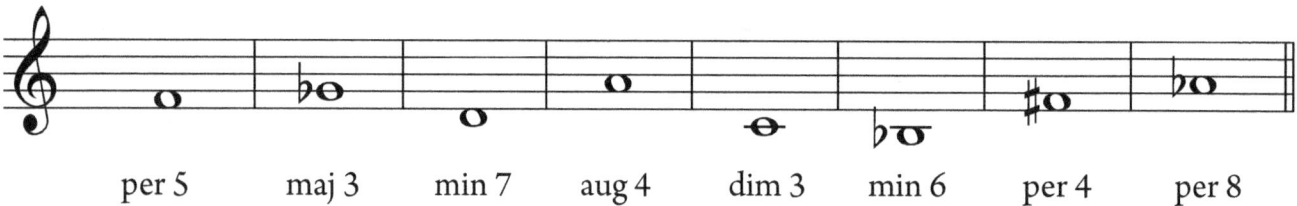

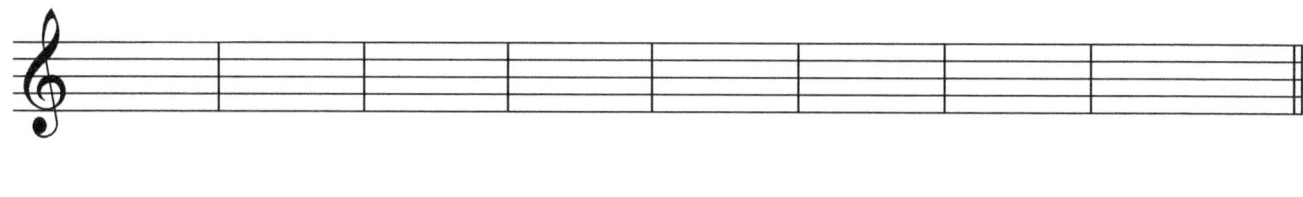

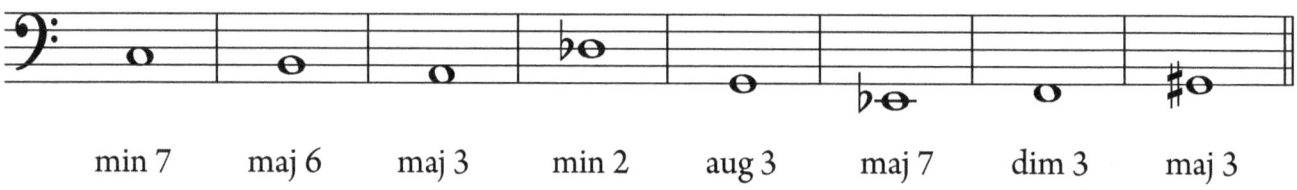

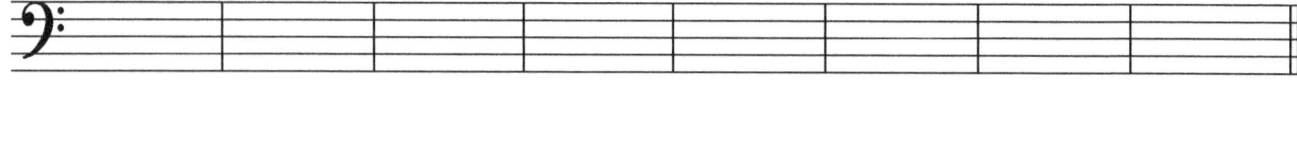

4. Name the following melodic intervals.

Frederic Chopin
Ballade, Op 23, No. 1

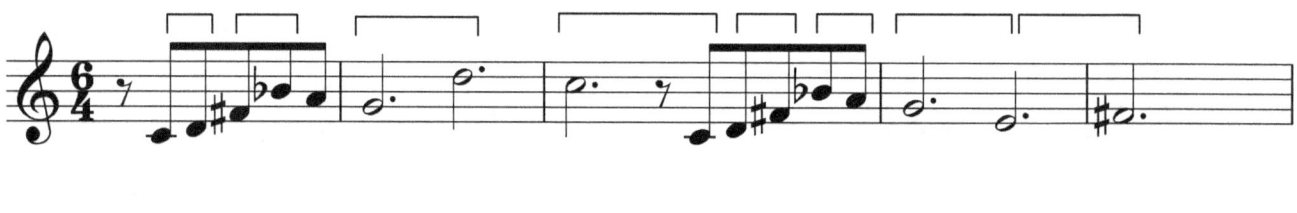

Enharmonic Change

If you change a note enharmonically, you change its name but not its pitch. Figure 8.8 shows enharmonic notes. Each measure contains two notes of the same pitch, but with a different name.

Figure 8.8

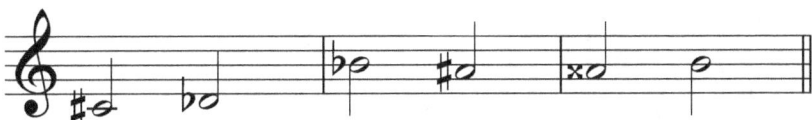

The intervals in each measure of Figure 8.9 sound exactly the same, but are named differently. The top note in example a) is changed enharmonically from B♭ to A♯, and the bottom note in example b) is changed enharmonically from A♭ to G♯. Even though the pitch does not change, the interval number and quality changes.

Figure 8.9

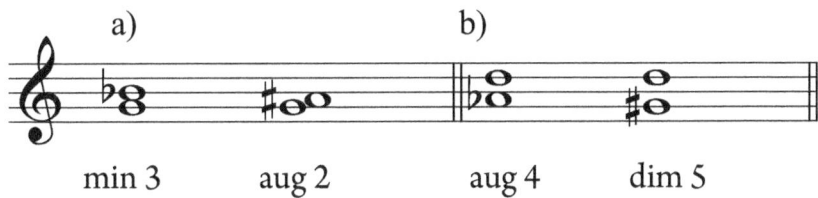

1. Name the following intervals. In the second measure change the lower note enharmonically and rename the interval. The first one is done for you.

dim 5   aug 4

2. Name the following intervals. In the second measure change the upper note enharmonically and rename the interval.

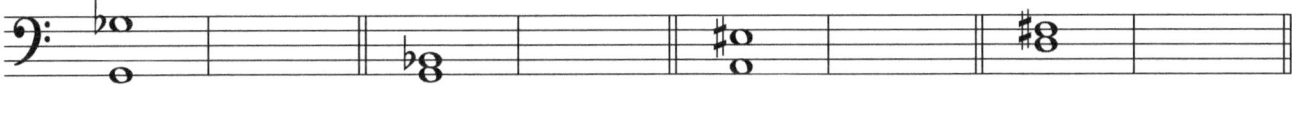

9
Rhythm and Meter

Dotted Notes

A dot placed just to the right of a note or rest increases its value by half. A whole note receives 4 beats. A dot beside it, adds half of that (2 beats), for a total of 6 beats. 4 + 2 = 6. Figure 9.1 contains dotted notes in quarter time. Dotted rests have the same values.

Figure 9.1

Dotted Whole Note 6 beats	𝅝·	=	𝅝	+ 𝅗𝅥
Dotted Half Note 3 beats	𝅗𝅥·	=	𝅗𝅥	+ 𝅘𝅥
Dotted Quarter Note 1 ½ beats	𝅘𝅥·	=	𝅘𝅥	+ 𝅘𝅥𝅮
Dotted Eighth Note ¾ beat	𝅘𝅥𝅮·	=	𝅘𝅥𝅮	+ 𝅘𝅥𝅯

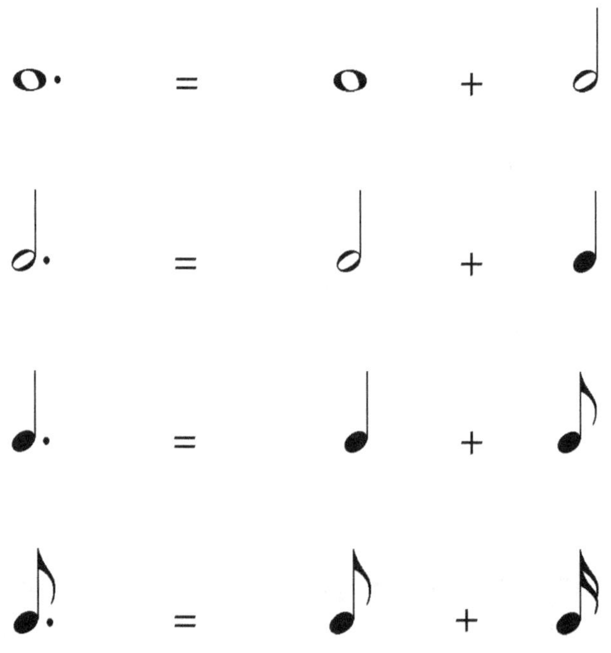

Double Dotted Notes

An additional dot may be added to an already dotted note or rest. The second dot increases the duration of the note or rest by half the value of the first dot. Figure 9.2 shows double dotted notes and equivalent values. Double dotted rests have the same values.

Figure 9.2

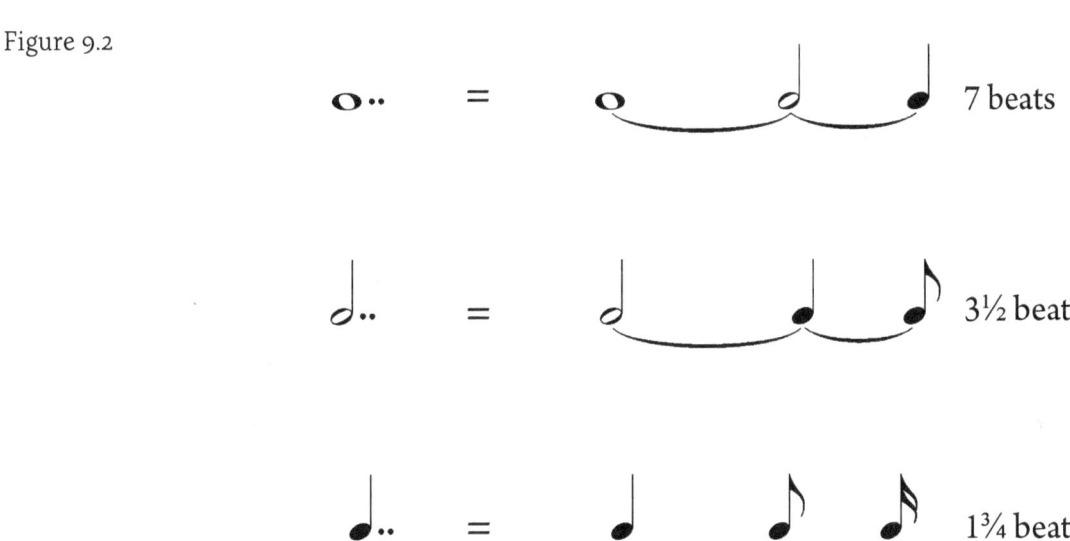

A double dotted note is usually followed by whatever note finishes the measure or the beat. Figure 9.3 illustrates this. Notice the double dotted eighth note in measure 2 which is worth ⅞ of a beat. This is usually joined with a thirty-second note to make one complete beat.

Figure 9.3

1. Complete the following:

   a. 1 eighth note equals _____ sixteenth notes.
   b. 1 dotted half note equals _____ quarter notes.
   c. 1 dotted eighth note equals _____ sixteenth notes.
   d. 1 dotted whole note equals _____ half notes.
   e. 1 dotted whole note equals _____ quarter notes.
   f. 1 double dotted quarter note equals _____ sixteenth notes.
   a. 1 double dotted whole note equals _____ quarter notes.
   b. 1 double dotted half note equals _____ eighth notes.

2. Write a single note which is equal to the the value of the following.

3. Write a single rest which is equal to the the value of the following.

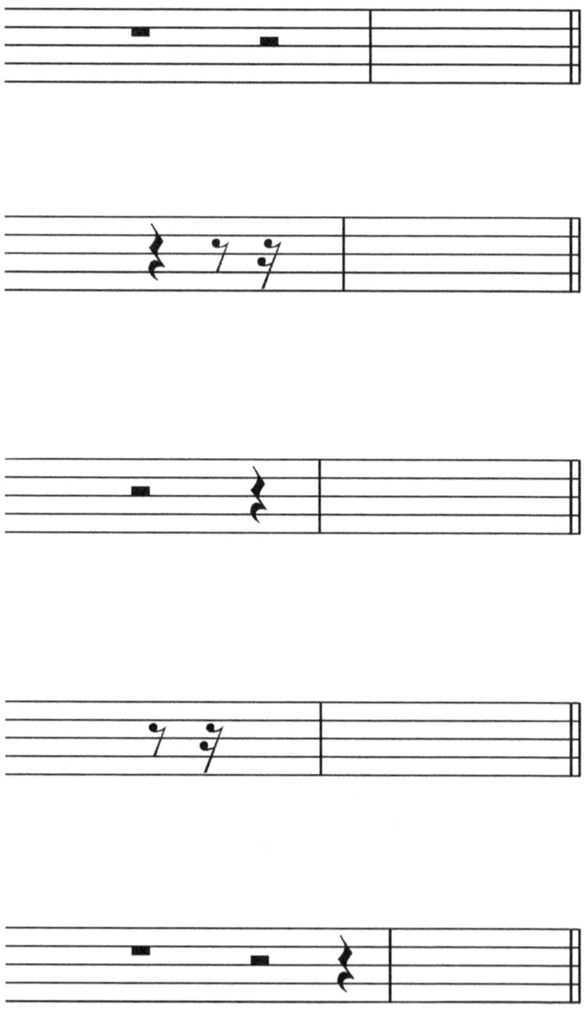

Rhythm and Meter

Simple and Compound Time

Simple time signatures divide the beat into two equal parts. Compound time signatures divide the beat into three equal parts.

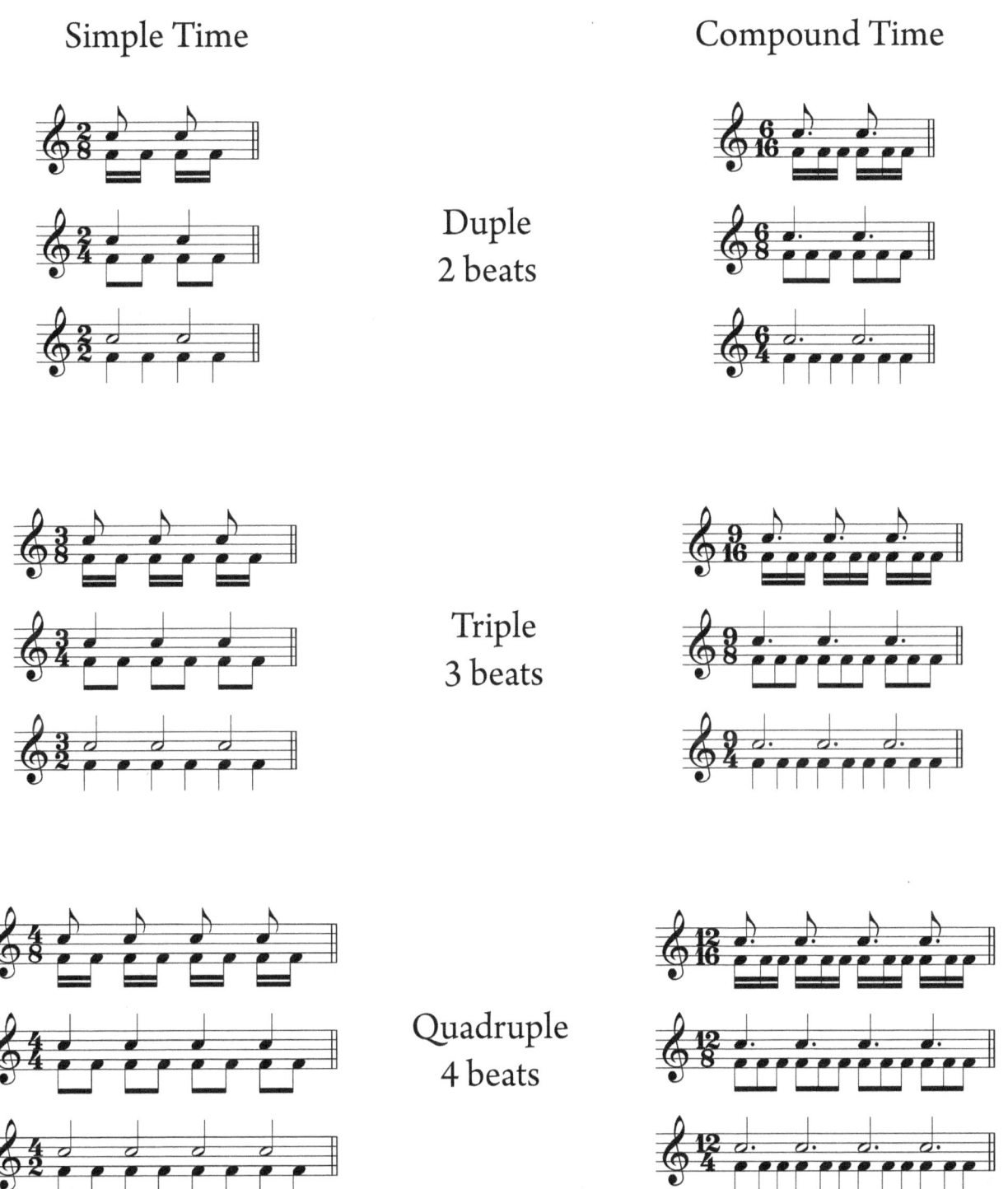

1. Add bar lines according to the time signatures.

Rhythm and Meter

2. Add time signatures at the beginning of each line.

Irregular Divisions of the Beat

A **tuplet** is the general name for a group of notes that do not follow the normal rules of counting. **Triplets, duplets, quadruplets, quintuplets, sextuplets,** and **septuplets** are all tuplets.

For review, a **triplet** is a group of three notes played in the time of two notes of the same value. Triplets generally occur in simple time Figure 9.4.

Figure 9.4

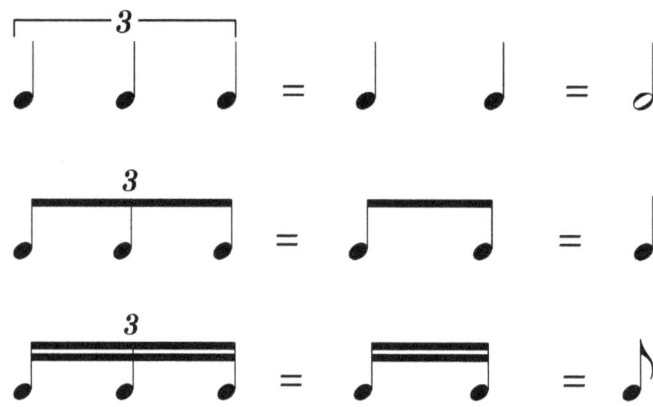

A **duplet** is a group of two notes played in the time of three notes of the same value. Duplets occur in compound time representing a group of three pulses or one beat Figure 9.5.

Figure 9.5

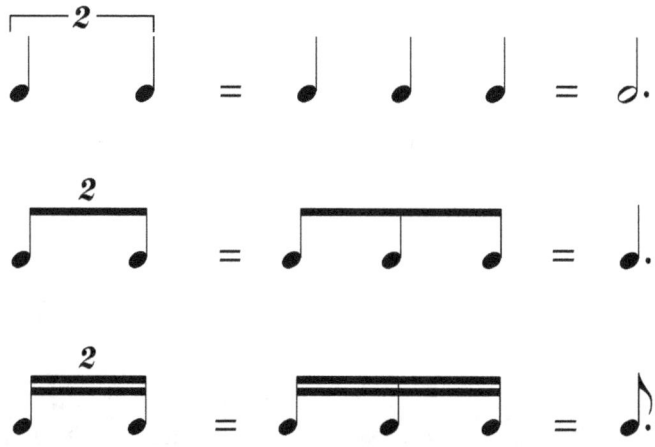

1. Add bar lines to the following according to the time signatures.

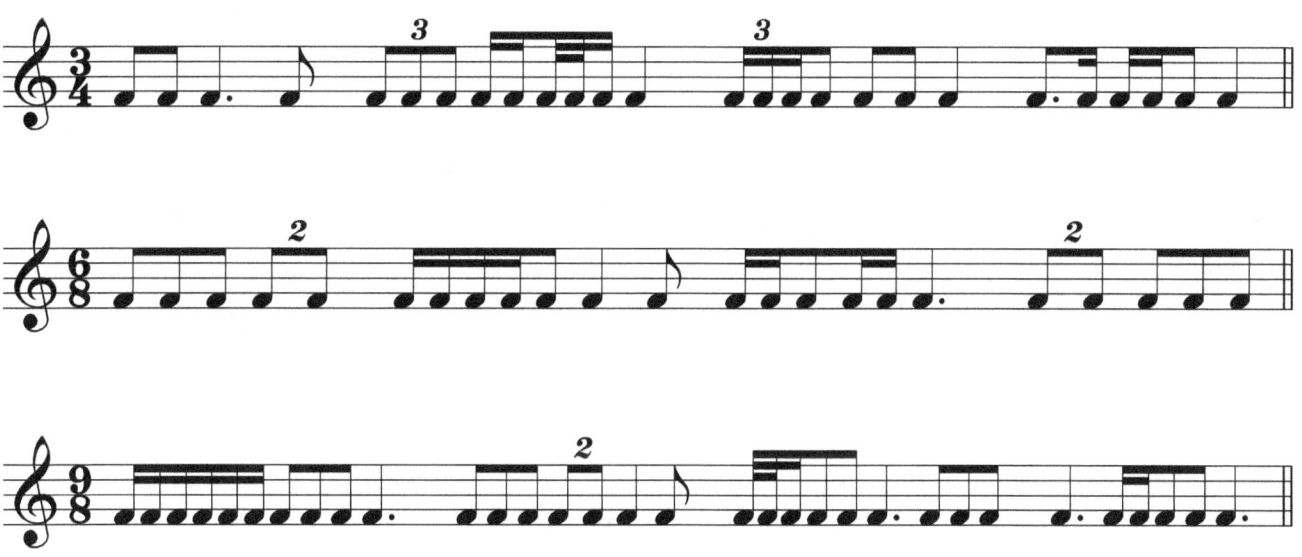

In simple time the beat may be divided into irregular groups of three, five, six or seven. A group of 5, 6, or 7 notes is played in the time of a group of 4 of the same kind in simple time.

Figure 9.6

In compound time the beat may be divided into irregular groups of two, four, five, or seven. In compound time the main beat is a dotted note. Each group represents one beat (three pulses). Some of the groups look the same in simple and compound time. To determine the beat in the melody with irregular groupings look at the time signature and the other beats in the bar.

Figure 9.7

Many composers used irregular groupings in their work. Figure 9.8 is an example of irregular groups in a composition by Tchaikowsky. Here, each group represents one beat in simple time.

Figure 9.8

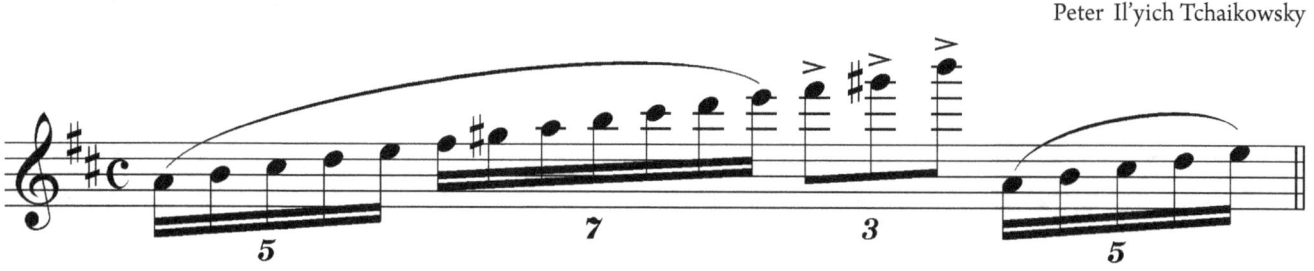

1. Add bar lines to the following excerpts which begin on the first beat of the bar.

Frédéric Chopin
Etude, Op. 10, No. 9

Frédéric Chopin
Waltz, Op. 69, No.1

Giacomo Puccini
Madam Butterfly (One Fine Day)

Lili Boulanger
Nocturne

Rests in Simple Time

A whole rest is used to indicate one complete measure of silence for every time signature except 4/2. In 4/2 meter, the double whole or breve rest is used to indicate a complete measure of silence Figure 9.9.

Figure 9.9

When adding rests to complete a measure of music it is important to show each beat clearly. In Figure 9.10 the first two measures contain one beat of music and are completed with one rest for the remaining beat. In the remaining two measures each incomplete beat is finished before moving on to the next beat.

Figure 9.10

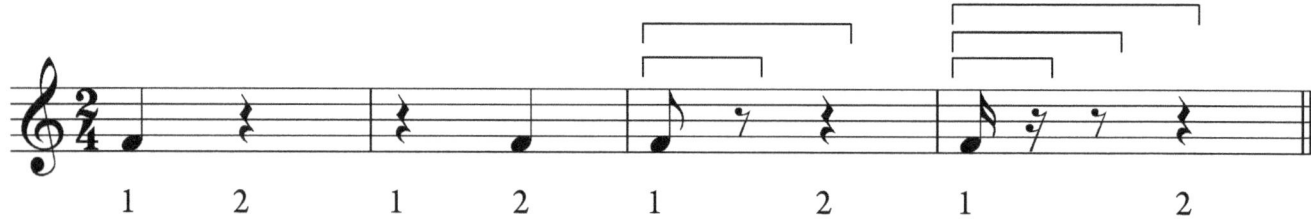

In simple triple meter never join beats two and three into one rest. Beats one and two may be joined or written as two separate rests Figure 9.11.

Figure 9.11

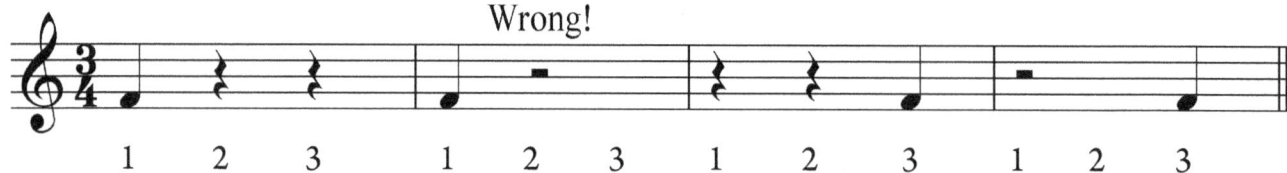

In simple quadruple meter join beats one and two into one rest and join beats three and four into one rest. Never join beats two and three into one rest Figure 9.12.

Figure 9.12

1. Add rests under the brackets to complete each measure.

Rests in Compound Time

Dotted rests are not used in simple meter. They are only used in compound meter and usually equal one beat. Two beats may be joined into one dotted rest to represent the first half or the last half of a measure in compound quadruple meter.

Figure 9.13

In compound meter each beat equals 3 pulses. The first 2 pulses of a beat should be joined into one rest as shown in Figure 9.14 a) and b). The last 2 pulses of a beat should use separate rests as shown in Figure 9.14 c) and d).

Figure 9.14

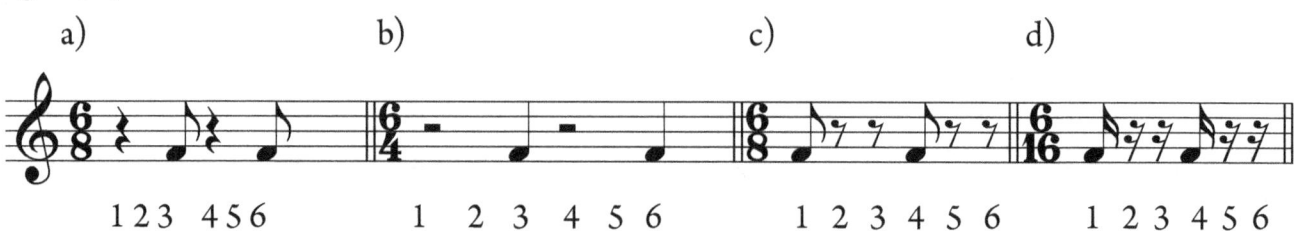

In compound triple meter beats 1 and 2 may be joined into one rest but do not join beats 2 and 3 into one rest.

Figure 9.15

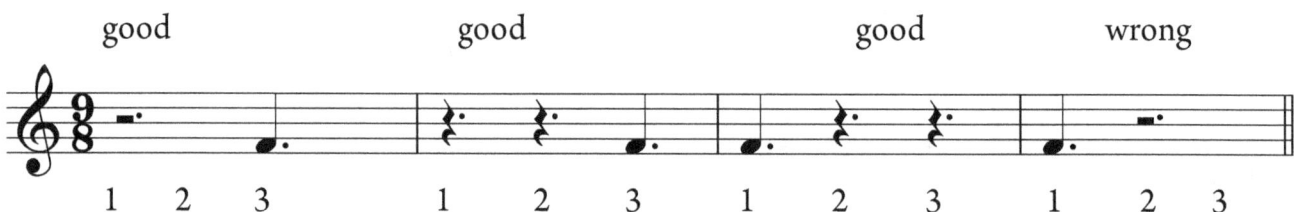

In compound quadruple time beats 1 and 2 should be joined into one rest. Beats 3 and 4 should be joined into one rest. Do not join beats 2 and 3 into one rest.

Figure 9.16

1. Add rests under the brackets to complete each measure.

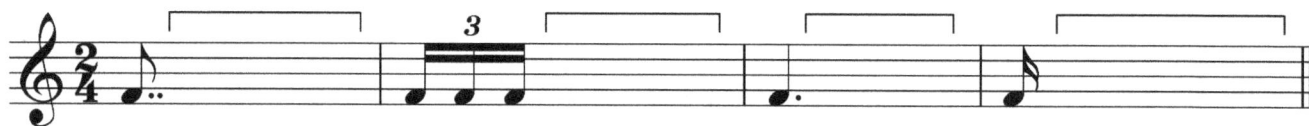

2. Add bar lines to the following excerpts which begin on the first beat of the bar.

Robert Schumann
Carnaval (Eusebius)

Franz Liszt
Hungarian Folksong No. 4

Johannes Brahms
Quintet Op. 111, II

10

Triads

Triad Qualities

The three notes of a triad are known as the root, third and fifth. The quality of a triad is determined by the intervals formed between the root and third and the root and fifth.

Figure 10.1 shows the four different triad qualities. Note the root/quality chord symbols.

Figure 10.1

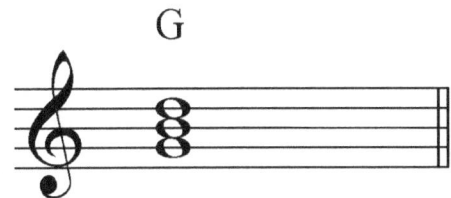

A *major triad* consist of the intervals of a major 3rd and a perfect 5th above the root.
        G to B is a major 3rd
        G to D is a perfect 5th

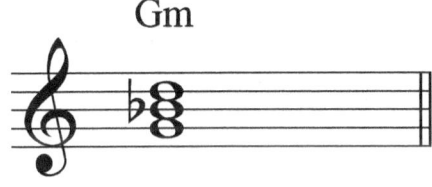

A *minor triad* consist of the intervals of a minor 3rd and a perfect 5th above the root.
        G to B♭ is a minor 3rd
        G to D is a perfect 5th

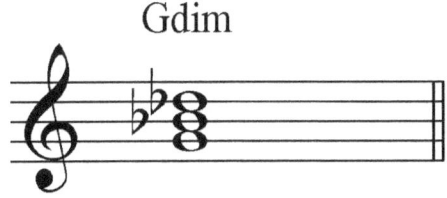

A *diminished triad* consist of the intervals of a minor 3rd and a diminished 5th above the root.
        G to B♭ is a minor 3rd
        G to D♭ is a diminished 5th

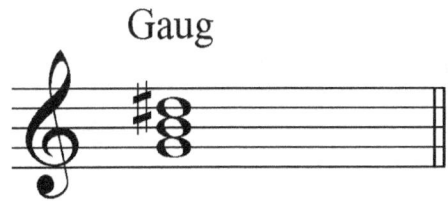

An *augmented triad* consist of the intervals of a major 3rd and an augmented 5th above the root.
        G to B is a major 3rd
        G to D♯ is an augmented 5th

©San Marco Publications 2022

1. Provide the root/quality chord symbols for the following triads.

2. Write diminished triads above the following notes.

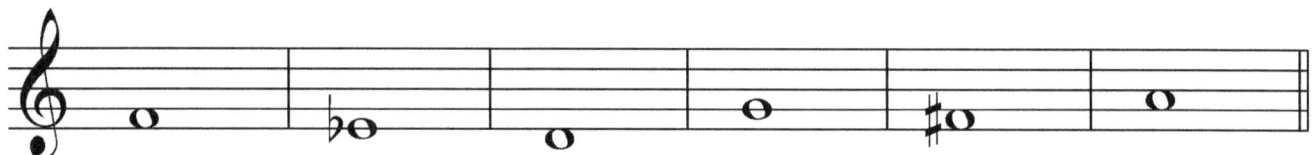

3. Write augmented triads above the following notes.

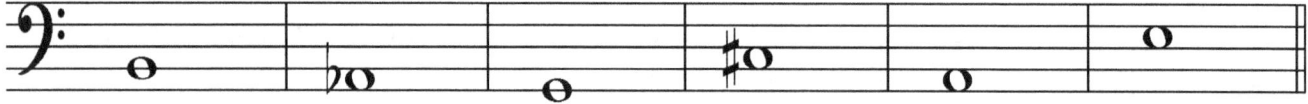

4. Identify the following triads as major, minor, augmented or diminished.

___   ___   ___   ___   ___   ___

Triad Inversions

Triads may appear in root position and two *inversions*. **Root position triads** have the root as the lowest note. **First inversion triads** have the 3rd as the lowest note. **Second inversion triads** have the 5th as the lowest note. Inverted chords can help make music more interesting. Inversions can create smoother motion between chords. They are used to make a bass line fluid and musical. This type of movement is called ***voice leading***. Using root position chords solely can make a disjunct, uneven bass line that jumps around too much. Inversions can make it smoother.

Figure 10.2 shows the three positions of the G major triad.

Figure 10.2

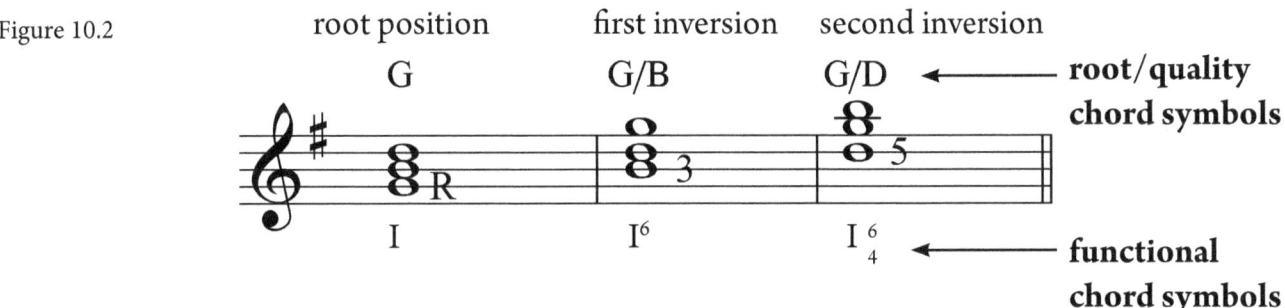

Solving Triads

Figure 10.3

Solving a triad involves stating its root, quality and position. To solve the triad in Figure 10.3:

1. If the triad is not in root position, put it into root position. Figure 10.4 shows that the root is **E**.

Figure 10.4

2. Determine the intervals between the root and 3rd and the root and 5th. In Figure 10.5 E to G is a minor 3rd and E to B♭ is a diminished 5th. This makes the chord quality **diminished**.

Figure 10.5

3. Examine the lowest note of the given triad. In Figure 10.3 it is the 3rd, G. When the 3rd is the lowest note, the position of the triad is **first inversion**. This triad is solved as follows:

Root: E
Quality: diminished
Position: 1st inversion

1. State the root, quality, and position for the following triads.

root: _____   _____   _____   _____   _____   _____
quality: _____   _____   _____   _____   _____   _____
position: _____   _____   _____   _____   _____   _____

root: _____   _____   _____   _____   _____   _____
quality: _____   _____   _____   _____   _____   _____
position: _____   _____   _____   _____   _____   _____

root: _____   _____   _____   _____   _____   _____
quality: _____   _____   _____   _____   _____   _____
position: _____   _____   _____   _____   _____   _____

2. Write the following triads.

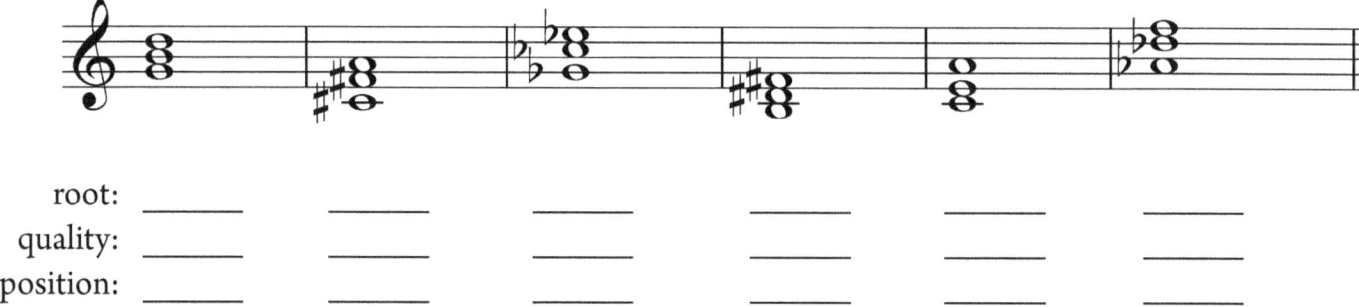

F major in root position G diminished in 1st inversion D minor in 2nd inversion C augmented in root position B♭ minor in 2nd inversion

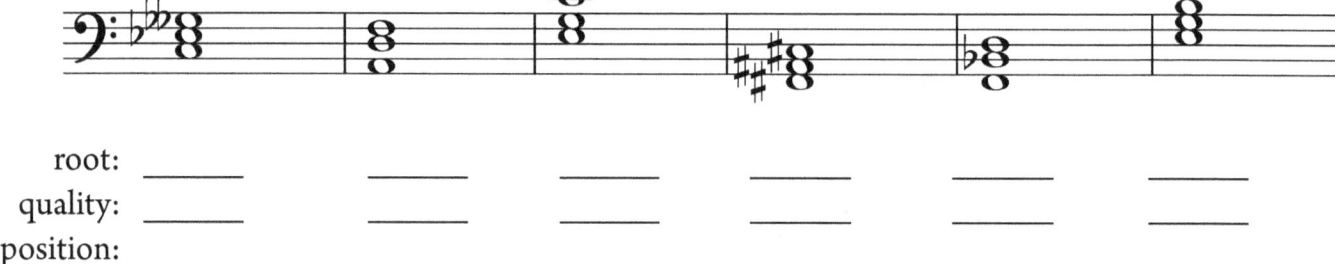

E major in root position A diminished in 1st inversion F♯ diminished in 2nd inversion B minor in root position B diminished in 1st inversion

Triads in Open Position

When a triad is written in open position, the notes of the triad are spaced out over more than an octave. Often, one of the notes of the triad is written more than once or **doubled**. The most common note to double is the root. The lowest note of the triad determines the position of the triad.

Figure 10.6 shows triads in open position with root/quality chord symbols.

Figure 10.6

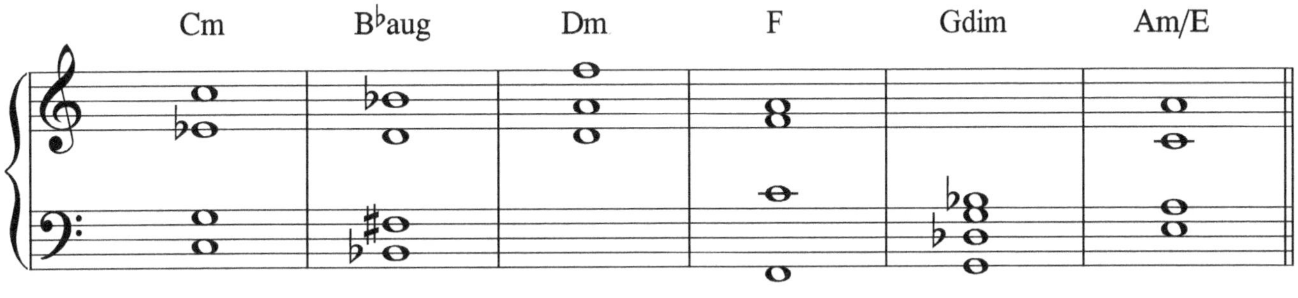

1. State the root, quality and position of the following triads. Add the root/quality chord symbol for each.

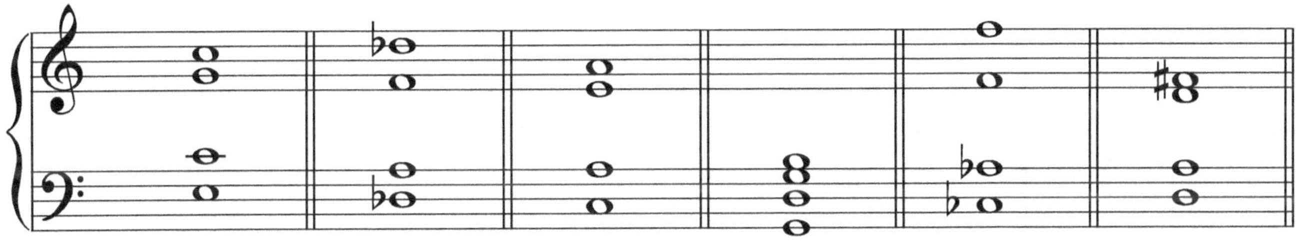

root: _____ _____ _____ _____ _____ _____
quality: _____ _____ _____ _____ _____ _____
position: _____ _____ _____ _____ _____ _____

root: _____ _____ _____ _____ _____ _____
quality: _____ _____ _____ _____ _____ _____
position: _____ _____ _____ _____ _____ _____

©San Marco Publications 2022

Triads Built on the Major and Minor Scale

Figure 10.7 illustrates the major, minor, and diminished triads that occur in the scale of C major. Each triad can be named for the scale degree on which it is built. The triad built on $\hat{1}$, the tonic, is considered the **tonic triad** in C major. The triad formed on $\hat{2}$, the supertonic, is considered the **supertonic triad** in C major. The triad built on $\hat{3}$ is the **mediant triad**, etc.

- The root/quality chord symbol for a major triad is an uppercase letter (C, G, etc.).
- The root/quality chord symbol for a minor triad is an uppercase letter and the letter m (Dm, Em, etc.).
- The root quality chord symbol for a diminished triad is the letter and "dim" (Bdim).
- The functional chord symbol a major triad is an uppercase Roman numeral (I, IV).
- The functional chord symbol for a minor triad is a lowercase Roman numeral (ii, iii).
- The functional chord symbol for a diminished triad is a lowercase case Roman numeral with the " ° " symbol (vii°).

Figure 10.7

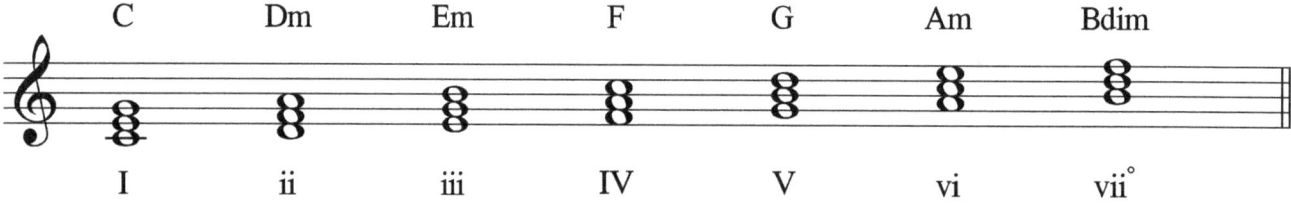

Major, minor, augmented and diminished triads occur in the harmonic minor scale. Figure 10.8 shows the triads on the A harmonic minor scale. Major triads occur on the dominant ($\hat{5}$) and the submediant ($\hat{6}$). Minor triads occur on the tonic ($\hat{1}$) and subdominant ($\hat{4}$). An augmented triad occurs on the mediant ($\hat{3}$). Diminished triads occur on the super tonic ($\hat{2}$) and the leading tone ($\hat{7}$). The raised leading tone is found in III⁺ and vii°.

- The root/quality chord symbol for an augmented triad is an uppercase letter and "aug" (Caug).
- The functional chord symbol for an augmented triad is an uppercase Roman numeral with the " + " symbol (III⁺).

Figure 10.8

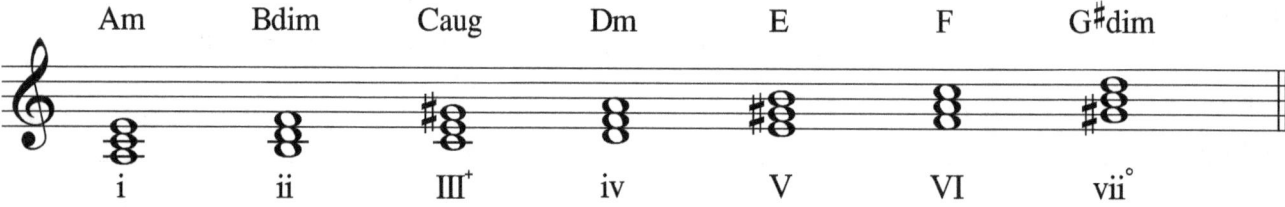

The following table summarizes the triads built on the scale degrees of the major and harmonic minor scales.

Triad	Major Scales	Harmonic Minor Scales
major	$\hat{1}$, $\hat{4}$, $\hat{5}$	$\hat{5}$, $\hat{6}$
minor	$\hat{2}$, $\hat{3}$, $\hat{6}$	$\hat{1}$, $\hat{4}$
diminished	$\hat{7}$	$\hat{2}$, $\hat{7}$
augmented	none	$\hat{3}$

Chord Symbols

Figure 10.9 contains two chords: the leading tone chord and its inversions in A minor, and the subdominant chord and its inversions in G major. Study the notation of the root/quality and functional chord symbols.

Figure 10.9

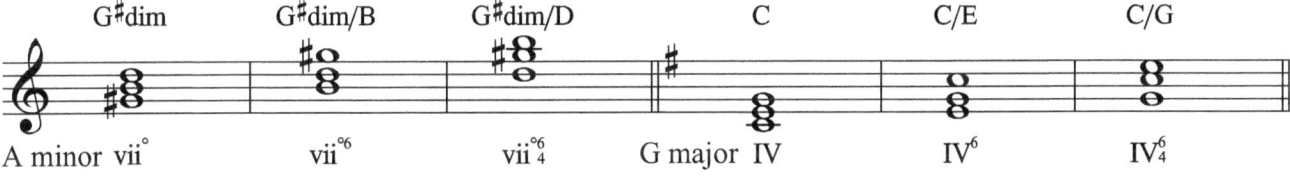

1. Write all the triads found on the F major scale. Add the functional and root/quality chord symbols for each.

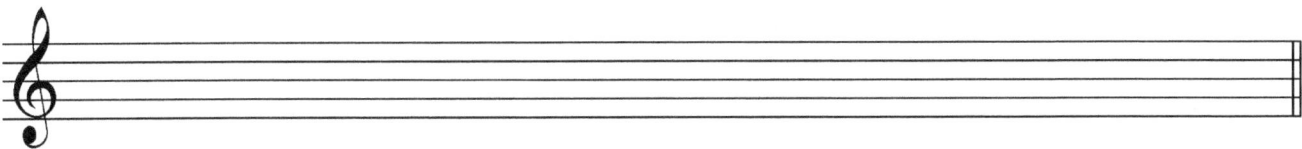

2. Write all the triads found on the D harmonic minor scale. Add the functional and root/quality chord symbols for each.

3. Name the major key for each triad. Write the scale degree name (tonic, mediant, etc.). Label each triad with functional and root/quality chord symbols.

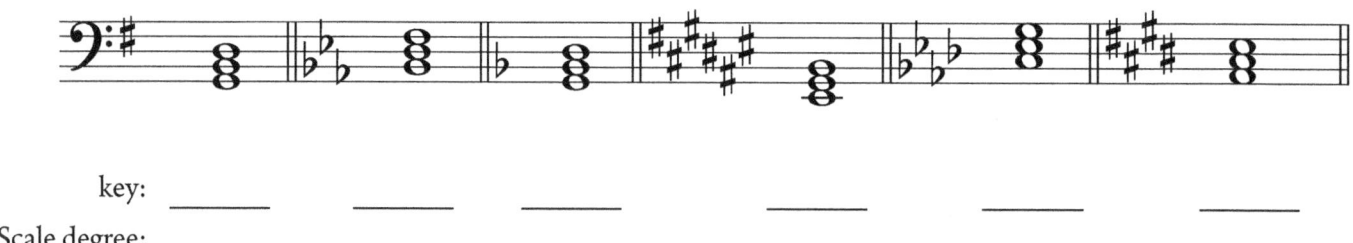

key: _____ _____ _____ _____ _____ _____
Scale degree: _____ _____ _____ _____ _____ _____

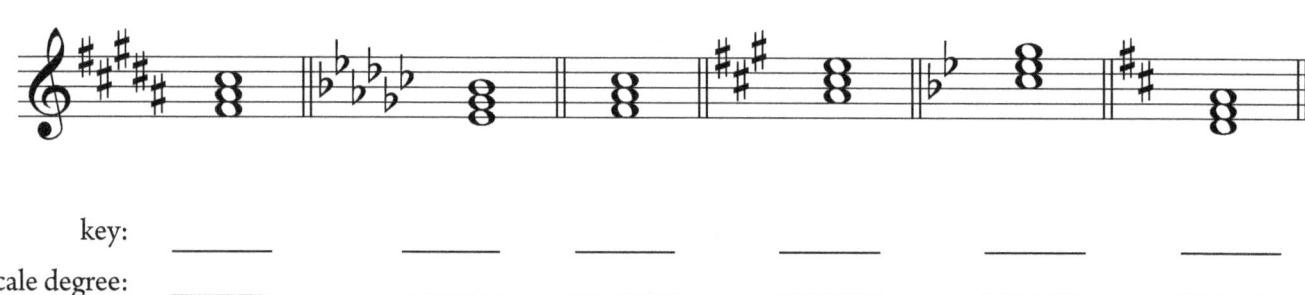

key: _____ _____ _____ _____ _____ _____
Scale degree: _____ _____ _____ _____ _____ _____

4. Name the minor key for each triad. Write the scale degree name (tonic, mediant, etc.). Label each triad with functional and root/quality chord symbols.

key: _____ _____ _____ _____ _____ _____
Scale degree: _____ _____ _____ _____ _____ _____

key: _____ _____ _____ _____ _____ _____
Scale degree: _____ _____ _____ _____ _____ _____

5. Write the following triads in close position using a key signature for each.

    i. The dominant triad of E harmonic minor in root position.
    ii. The mediant triad of E♭ major in first inversion.
    iii. The supertonic triad of F♯ harmonic minor in second inversion.
    iv. The subdominant triad of B major in root position.
    v. The dominant triad of G harmonic minor in first inversion.
    vi. The submediant triad of F major in root position.

    i.   ii.   iii.   iv.   v.   vi.

6. Write the following triads in close position using accidentals for each. Add the root/quality and functional chord symbols for each chord.

    i. The leading tone triad of B♭ harmonic minor in root position.
    ii. The submediant triad of F♯ major in second inversion.
    iii. The tonic triad of E♭ harmonic minor in first inversion.
    iv. The dominant triad of F harmonic minor in root position.
    v. The supertonic triad of E harmonic minor in first inversion.
    vi. The subdominant triad of D major in root position.

    i.   ii.   iii.   iv.   v.   vi.

7. Write a diminished triad in root position that can be found in the following scales. Use key signatures. Add the root/quality chord symbol to each chord.

i. C major   ii. G major   iii. E harmonic minor   iv. A♭ major   v. A harmonic minor   vi. E major

i.   ii.   iii.   iv.   v.   vi.

11

History 2

Frédéric Chopin (1810 - 1849)

Frédéric Chopin was born on March 1, 1810, in Żelazowa Wola, Poland. His father was French, and his mother was Polish. His mother introduced him to the piano. He started his musical education at 6, composed his first work at 7, and made his first appearance on stage at 8 years of age. Chopin was devoted to the piano and composed almost exclusively for this instrument.

When Chopin was 20, he left Poland for France and lived the rest of his life in Paris. However, his love and devotion for Poland never died. He carried a small silver box filled with Polish earth when he left Poland. This box was buried with him when he died in Paris in 1849. His heart was put in an urn and placed in the Church of the Holy Cross in Warsaw, Poland.

Chopin's music is infused with his love and devotion to Poland. Some of this influence can be seen in his piano works. He wrote mazurkas and polonaises, based on Polish folk dances.

The majority of his solo pieces are composed in smaller forms and have an improvisatory sound. These include 20 nocturnes, 25 preludes, 17 waltzes, 15 polonaises, 58 mazurkas and 27 etudes. Chopin also wrote larger forms, including the scherzo, the ballade (a genre he invented), and the sonata. The four Ballades and the two Sonatas are among his most significant compositions.

Chopin had a love for opera and the music of opera composer Vincenzo Bellini. Much of his piano music is written in a style called *bel canto*. Bel Canto style translates to "beautiful singing style." Chopin's piano music is noted for its beautiful singing lines and melodies. His music is also known for its virtuosity and its advanced treatment of harmony and rhythm.

Elements in Chopin's Music

Rubato: All of Chopin's music employs rubato. This is an expressive and rhythmic freedom achieved by speeding up and slowing down the tempo of a piece at the discretion of the performer.

Harmony: Unlike composers of the past, Chopin's chords don't just function as a set of tensions and resolutions. Many have a unique, individual, colorful sound. Chopin discovered that dissonance, which creates tension and traditionally requires resolution, can be beautiful by itself. His music often contains chromaticism, unusual modulations, and sudden key changes.

Nationalism: Music based on a composers country is nationalistic. Polish culture, folk songs, and rhythms influence Chopin's music.

Etude Op. 10 No. 12 (Revolutionary)

The term *etude* is used to describe a piece of music that focuses on refining and training a specific aspect of a performers technique. Etudes are sometimes referred to as *studies*. Many etudes are just repetitions of note patterns and lack real musicality. Chopin's etudes are different. He was the first composer to pioneer the etude as an actual art form. He wrote 27 etudes for piano. Each of the Chopin etudes not only trains a specific technical area but also tells an emotional story. They are anything but repetitive, dry, technical exercises. This musical approach to the etude continued through the Romantic period and other composers, notably Franz Liszt, wrote in this genre.

Chopin's etudes cover many areas of technique, from arpeggios to octaves, but all are designed to develop a legato style of playing.

The Etude in C minor Op. 10, No. 12 is one of Chopin's most recognized compositions. The genre of this etude is *solo piano piece*. This piece has been given the programmatic title "Revolutionary Etude." It was composed after Chopin heard of Poland's failure in its rebellion against Russia. Chopin never gave titles like this to his compositions, almost always preferring to refer to them by opus and number. He probably did not come up with this title, and actually may have disapproved of it. This nickname might be attributed to an editor or fan of his music.

Most of the technical difficulty in this etude is in the left hand, which has rapid runs, arpeggios, and broken chords. It is in ternary (ABA) form.

A is mm. 1 - 28
B is mm. 29 - 42
A is mm. 43 - 84

The opening eight measures act as in introduction to the main theme which begins in m. 10 (Figure 11.1).

Figure 11.1

Find and listen to a recording of this etude on the internet.

Music Terms and Signs

Study the following Italian terms and their meanings.

quindicesima alta, 15ma	play 2 octaves higher
semplice	simple
sonore	sonorous, resonant; with rich tone
sopra	above, indicates piano player crossing hands
tacet	be silent, voice or instrument does not play
tutti	a passage for the whole ensemble
volta	time, *prima volta*=1st time, *seconda volta*=2nd time
volti subito, v.s.	turn the page quickly

glissando, gliss a continuous sliding up or down from one pitch to another

12

Seventh Chords

The Dominant Seventh Chord - Review

Seventh chords are very common in Western music, and we hear them all the time.

One of the most common seventh chords is the ***dominant seventh***. The functional chord symbol for the dominant seventh is V^7. This means that the chord is built on scale degree $\hat{5}$ (the dominant) and contains the interval of a seventh above the root. A dominant 7th chord contains four notes, the root, 3rd, 5th, and 7th. V^7 is a major triad with a minor 7th above the root. In other words, the intervals above the root are a major 3rd, perfect 5th, and a minor 7th.

V^7 contains certain notes, like the leading tone that pull our ear toward the tonic chord.

Figure 12.1 shows V^7 chords in C and G major and D and E minor. When a key signature is used for these chords, the seventh of V^7 is automatically a minor seventh. In minor keys, V^7 like V contains raised $\hat{7}$.

Figure 12.1

Dominant seventh chords sound the same in tonic major and minor keys.

Figure 12.2 shows the dominant seventh chords in F major and F minor. Even though the notation is different, they sound the same and are made up of the same notes.

Figure 12.2

F major   V⁷   F minor   V⁷

1. Name the key and write the functional and root/quality chord symbols for the following dominant seventh chords.

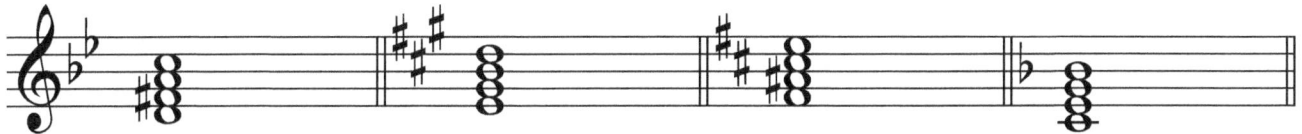

Inversions of the Dominant Seventh

V^7 occurs in root position and three inversions. These are shown in Figure 12.3. Study the root/quality chord symbols.

- If the root is the lowest note, V^7 is in **root position**.
- If the 3rd is the lowest note, V^7 is in **1st inversion**.
- If the 5th is the lowest note, V^7 is is **2nd inversion**.
- If the 7th is the lowest note, V^7 is in **3rd inversion**.

Figure 12.3

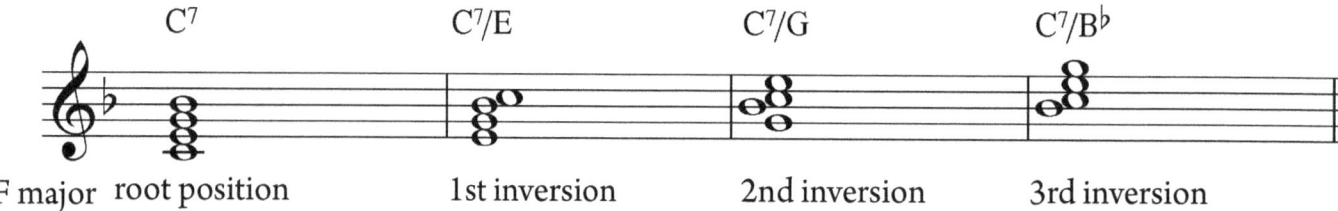

When writing the functional chord symbols for inversions of V^7, some of the numbers are omitted.

Figure 12.4 shows the numbers that indicate the intervals that occur above the lowest note. The lower chord symbols are the actual chord symbols that are used for V^7 and its inversions.

Figure 12.4

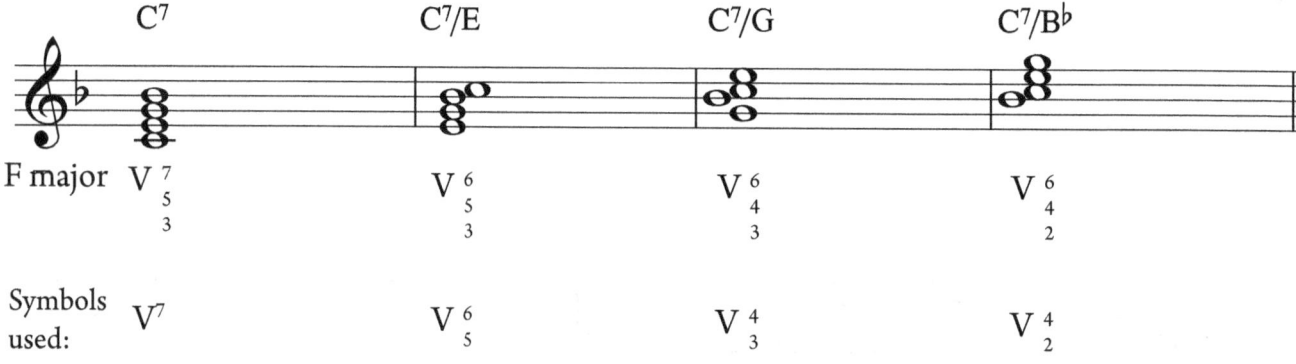

©San Marco Publications 2022

Seventh Chords

1. Write dominant seventh chords and their inversion in the following keys using a key signature for each.

G major

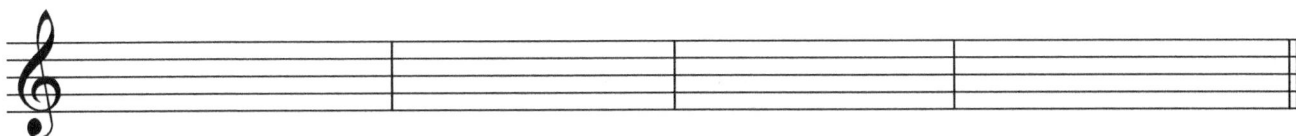

C minor

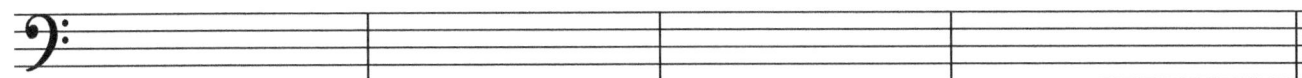

B major

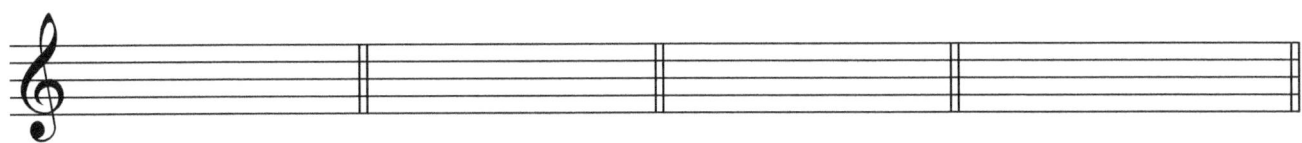

E minor

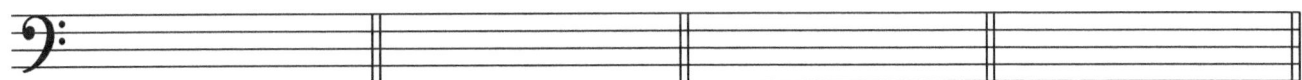

2. Solve the following dominant chords by stating the two keys, root and position for each.

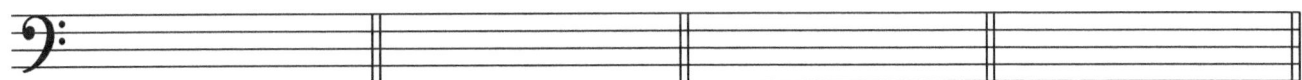

root: _____ _____ _____ _____ _____ _____
key: _____ _____ _____ _____ _____ _____
key: _____ _____ _____ _____ _____ _____
position: _____ _____ _____ _____ _____ _____

Seventh Chords

root: _____ _____ _____ _____ _____ _____
key: _____ _____ _____ _____ _____ _____
key: _____ _____ _____ _____ _____ _____
position: _____ _____ _____ _____ _____ _____

3. Add accidentals to the following to make dominant seventh chords. Name the major key for each.

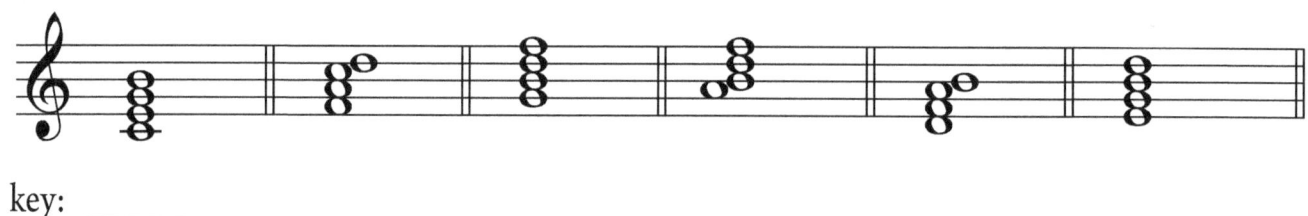

key: _____ _____ _____ _____ _____ _____

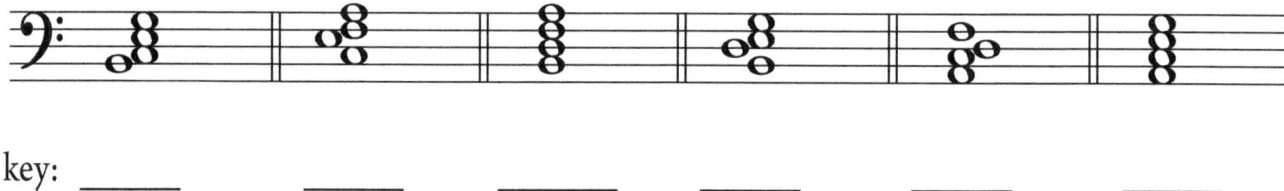

key: _____ _____ _____ _____ _____ _____

4. State the root, key, and position of the following dominant seventh chords.

root: _____ _____ _____ _____ _____ _____
key: _____ _____ _____ _____ _____ _____
position: _____ _____ _____ _____ _____ _____

root: _____ _____ _____ _____ _____ _____
key: _____ _____ _____ _____ _____ _____
position: _____ _____ _____ _____ _____ _____

The Diminished Seventh Chord

The ***diminished seventh chord*** is built on raised $\hat{7}$ in the minor key.

Figure 12.5 contains the diminished seventh built on raised $\hat{7}$ in A minor. The functional chord symbol is vii°⁷.

Figure 12.5

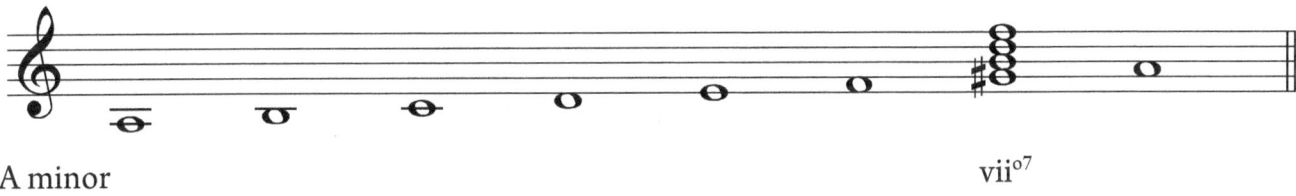

A minor   vii°⁷

Figure 12.6 shows that this chord consists of a diminished triad with the interval of a diminished 7th above the root of the chord. The root/quality symbol is G♯dim⁷ or G♯°⁷.

Figure 12.6

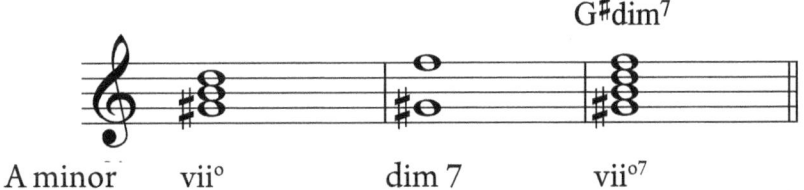

A minor   vii°   dim 7   vii°⁷

1. Name the key and write the functional and root/quality chord symbols for the following diminished 7th chords.

Symbol:

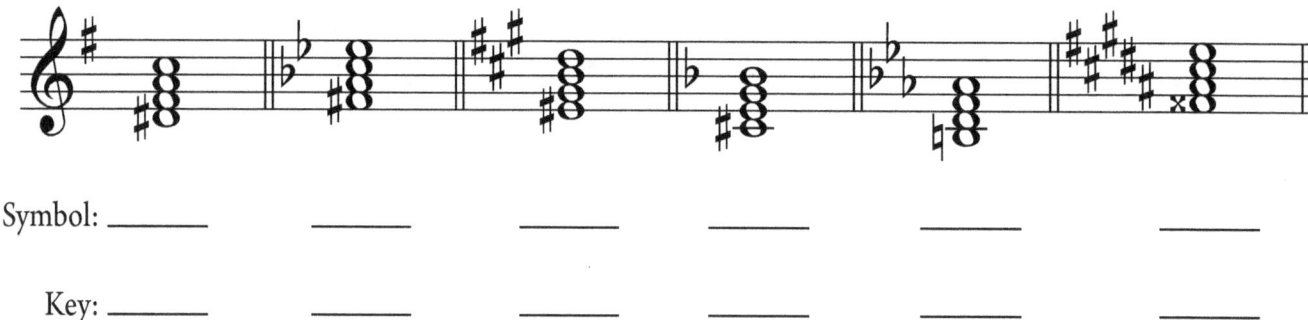

Symbol: _____   _____   _____   _____   _____   _____

Key: _____   _____   _____   _____   _____   _____

2. Write diminished 7th chords in the following keys using a key signature for each.

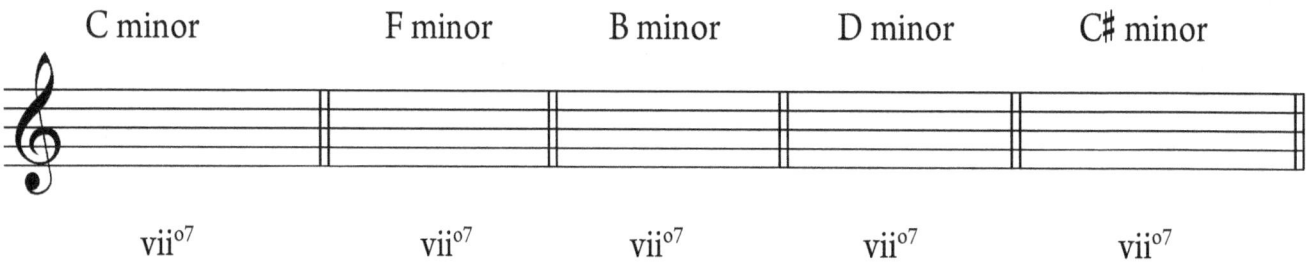

Review 2

1. Name the following intervals. Change the lower note enharmonically and rename them.

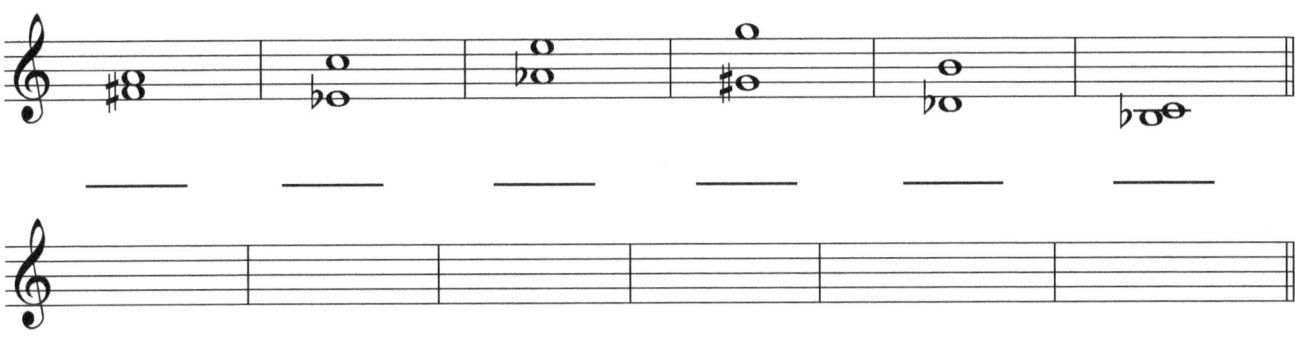

2. Write the following intervals above the given notes. Invert them and rename them.

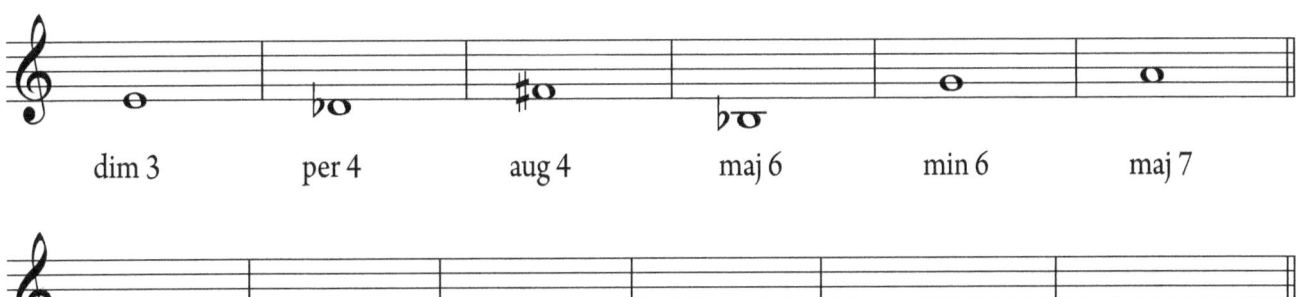

dim 3   per 4   aug 4   maj 6   min 6   maj 7

3. Add rests under the backets to complete each measure.

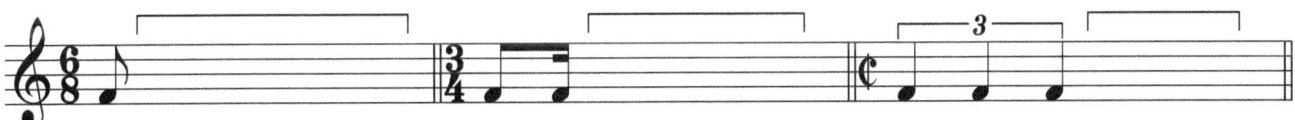

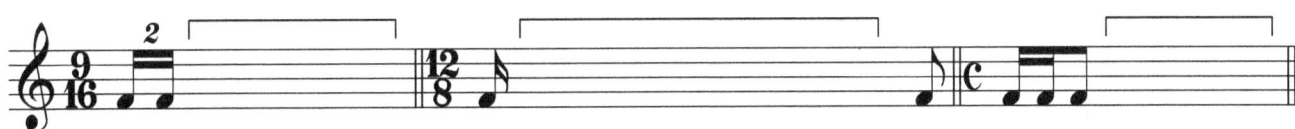

4. Define the following Italian terms.

martellato _____

morendo _____

pesante _____

scherzando _____

5. Write the following dominant 7th chords in close position using key signatures.

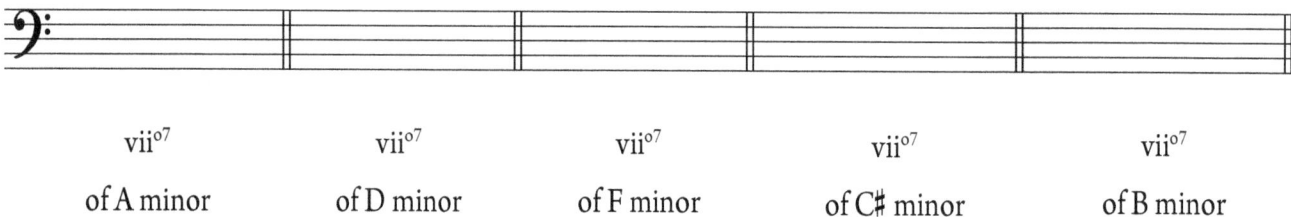

| V^7 | V^6_5 | V^7 | V^4_2 | V^4_3 |
| of A major | of C minor | of D♭ major | of E minor | of F major |

6. Write the following leading tone diminished 7th chords in root position using key signatures.

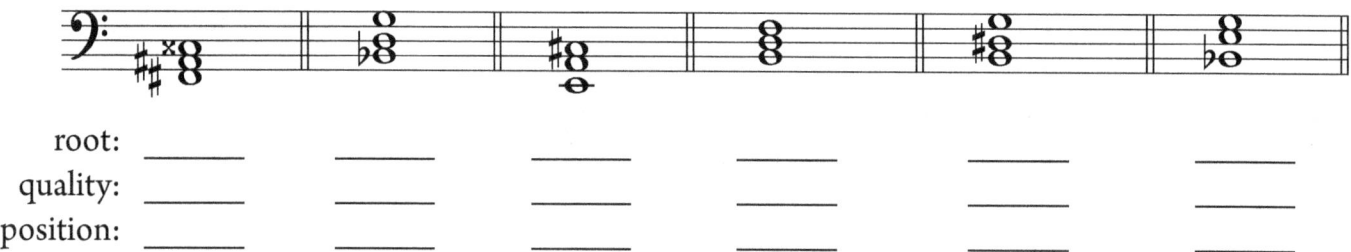

| vii^{o7} | vii^{o7} | vii^{o7} | vii^{o7} | vii^{o7} |
| of A minor | of D minor | of F minor | of C♯ minor | of B minor |

7. Identify the root, quality, and position of the following triads.

root: _____ _____ _____ _____ _____ _____
quality: _____ _____ _____ _____ _____ _____
position: _____ _____ _____ _____ _____ _____

8. Answer true (T) or false (F) to the following statements.

a. Frédéric Chopin was born in France. _____

b. Chopin composed in the classical era. _____

c. Chopin composed mainly for the piano. _____

d. Chopin wrote in 'bel canto style.' _____

e. 'Nationalism' refers to music with a pictorial or literary association. _____

f. 'Rubato' refers to music from Poland. _____

g. 'Etudes' are sometimes referred to as studies. _____

h. Chopin's Revolutionary Etude is in C minor. _____

13
Cadences

Music is divided into sections or units of various lengths called *phrases*. A phrase is a musical idea, much like a sentence in a story. Most phrases in traditional music are four measures long. A phrase ends with a *cadence*, which is a place of rest in music. A cadence is like the period at the end of a sentence. Cadences consist of two chords which bring a phrase to a close.

There are two types of cadences: *final* and *non-final*. Final cadences bring a phrase to a complete ending. Non-final cadences look forward and do not complete a musical idea. These cadences need another phrase to complete their non-final character.

Figure 13.1 contains two phrases from a Mozart Rondo with a cadence at the end of each. Play this example and listen to the cadences.

Figure 13.1

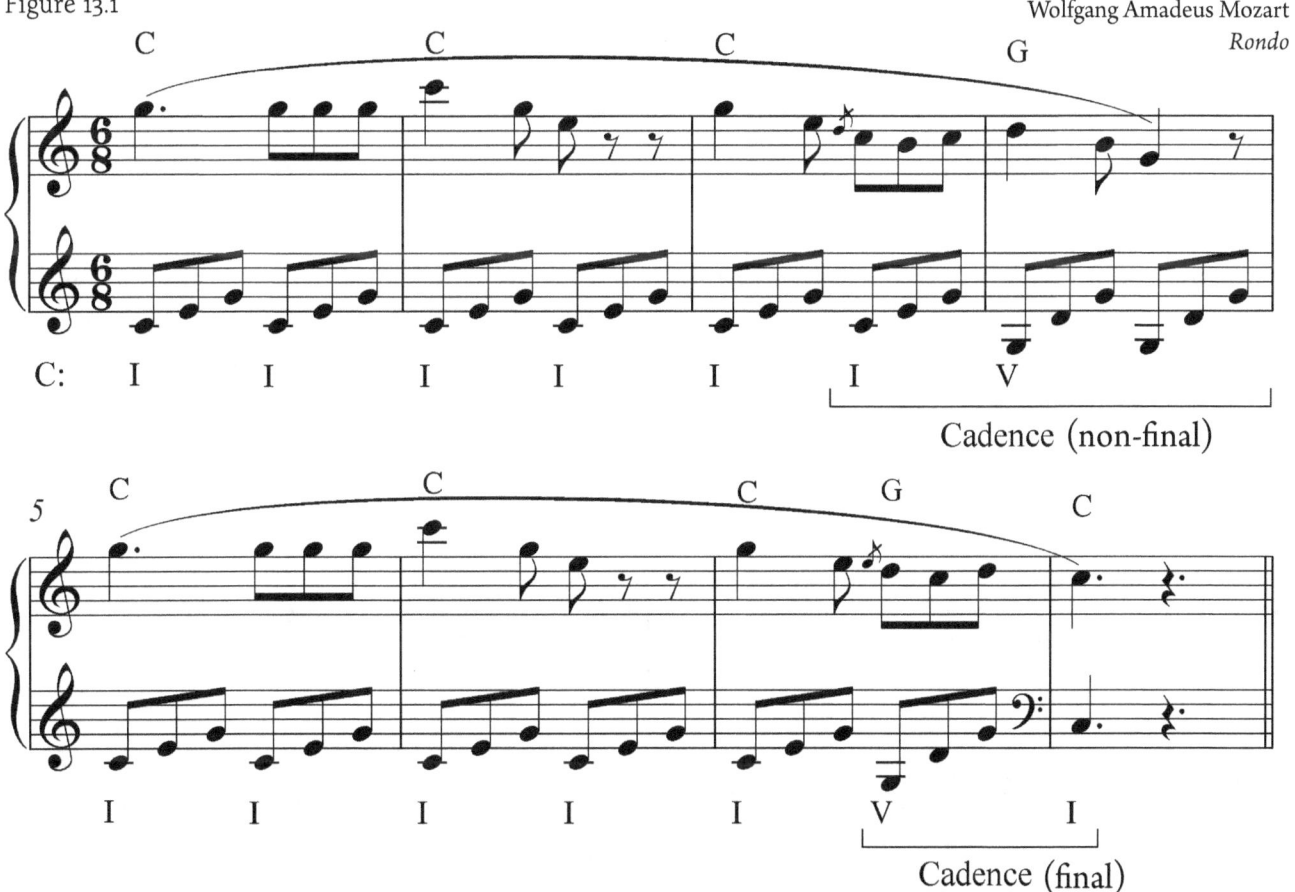

Wolfgang Amadeus Mozart
Rondo

The Authentic Cadence

The most frequently used final cadence is the ***authentic cadence***. It is the strongest and most conclusive cadence. It consists of the chords V - I or V - i (in minor keys). Figure 13.2 contains two authentic cadences in keyboard style. Notice the following common features of these cadences:

- They occur on the last two notes of the phrase.
- The first chord is on a weaker beat than the second chord.
- The V chord in a minor key contains raised $\hat{7}$.
- In keyboard style, three notes of the chord are placed on the treble staff, and the root of each chord is in the bass staff.
- These cadences are considered ***perfect authentic cadences*** because they end with the tonic as the top note of the I chord. In the D major cadence, D is the final and top note. In the E minor cadence, E is the final and top note. Ending on the tonic confirms the key and gives the cadence a strong final sound.

Figure 13.2

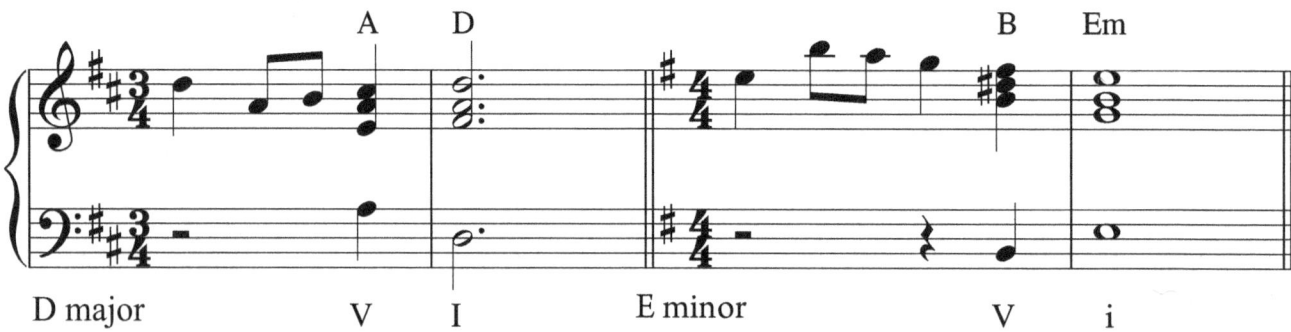

The cadences in Figure 13.3 are considered ***imperfect authentic cadences*** because they end with a note other than the tonic on top. The D major cadence ends with the 5th (A) as the final and top note. The E minor cadence ends on the 3rd (G) as the final and top note. These are still final cadences but do not sound as strong and final as a perfect authentic cadence which ends with the tonic as the final and top note.

Figure 13.3

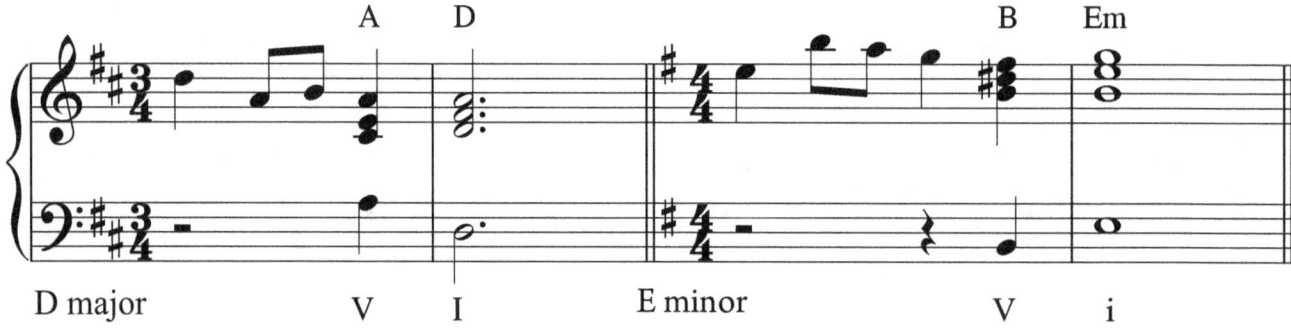

V^7 - I is an authentic cadence. Figure 13.4 contains two authentic cadences using V^7. In the first example in G major, the V^7 chord is complete using all four notes, D F♯ A C. In the D minor example the V^7 chord is considered incomplete. In this cadence the root is doubled, and the 5th of the chord is left out, A C♯ G A. Both examples are correct. The root of each chord must always be in the bass.

Figure 13.4

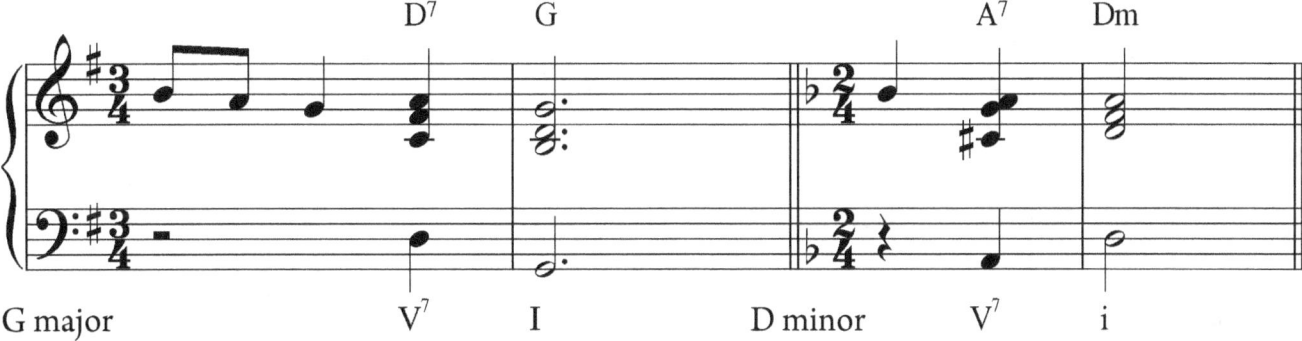

The Half Cadence

The *half cadence* is a non-final cadence. It ends with the V chord. Ending a phrase on the V chord leaves the music with an open or unfinished sound. For this reason, a piece of music does not end with a half cadence. Half cadences always end on V and never the dominant seventh, since V^7 contains too many strong tones that do not allow a feeling of rest. We will study two half cadences that are shown in Figure 13.5. These two cadences are I - V and IV - V.

Figure 13.5

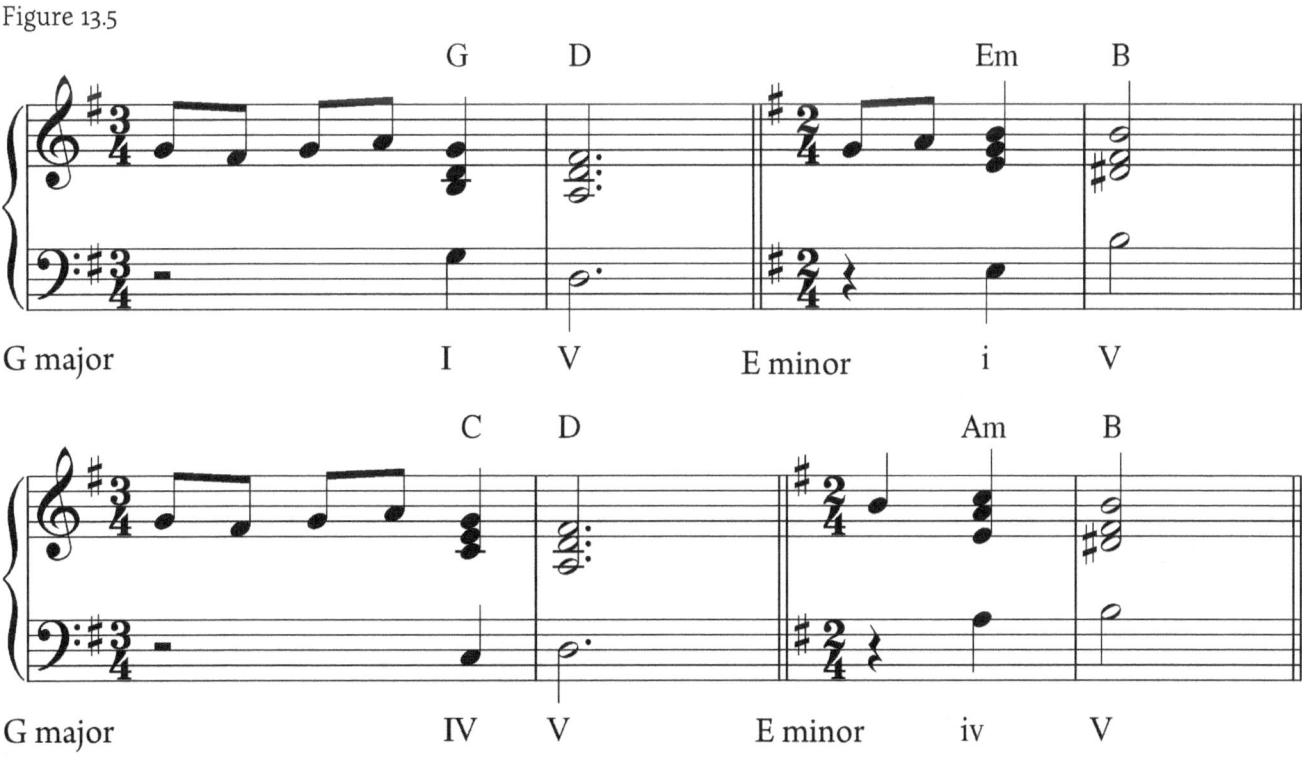

1. For the following cadences: Name the key, write the functional and root/quality chord symbols and name them as half, perfect authentic, or imperfect authentic.

Writing Cadences

Certain guidelines should be followed when writing cadences. Study the following steps for writing an authentic cadence in E minor.

1. Add the key signature and rests at the beginning of the first measure. Cadences often occur over the bar line with the second chord of the cadence on a stronger beat than the first. The first chord usually occurs in the second half or second part of the first measure on a weaker beat. In Figure 13.6 the key signature of E minor is F sharp. It is placed *before* the time signature. Roman numerals indicating the functional chord symbols of the authentic cadence are placed under the staff (V - i). Since this is 3/4 time a half rest is used at the beginning of the measure and the V chord will be placed on beat 3 of the first measure. There are other options that could be used for rhythm here, but this is effective.

Figure 13.6

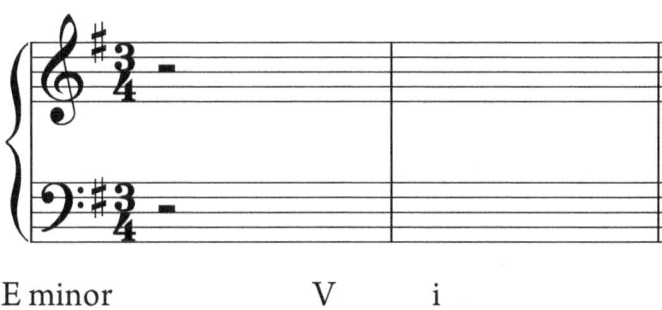

2. Write the bass notes for the V and the i chords. In E minor the root of V is B, and the root of i is E. In Figure 13.7 they are written as a quarter note (B) to complete the first measure, and a dotted half note (E) to complete the second measure.

Figure 13.7

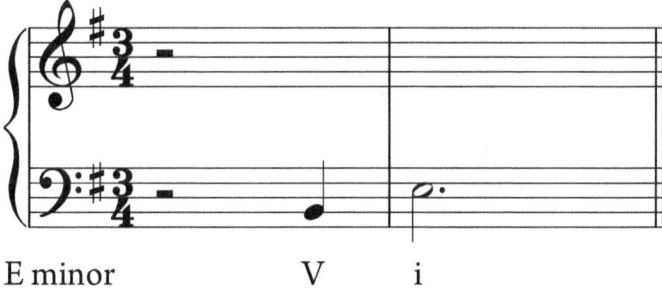

3. Write the notes of the V chord in close position on the treble staff. Close position occurs when the notes of the triad are as close together as possible. In E minor V is B-D♯-F♯. These notes can be in any order as long as they stay in close position. Figure 13.8 uses quarter notes on beat 3 of the first measure for this chord.

Figure 13.8

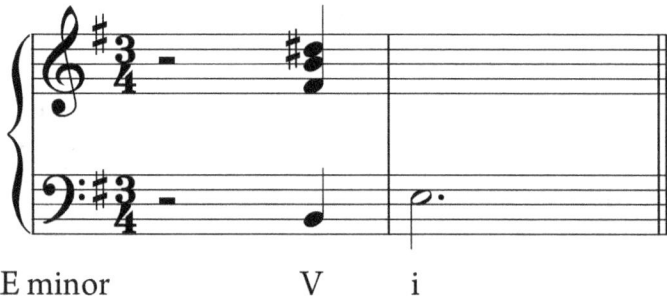

E minor   V   i

4. Write the notes of the i chord in the second measure. i in E minor is E-G-B. Keep these notes as close as possible to the notes of the V chord. In Figure 13.9 there is one note that is common to both chords (B). This B is kept in the same place in both chords (here it is the middle note). This note is called the **common tone**. Repeating the common tone in the same place creates smooth movement. This movement of notes from chord to chord is called **voice leading**. The leading tone (D♯) rises to the tonic (E). If the leading tone is at the top of the chord, it should rise to the tonic. The F♯ steps up to G.

Figure 13.9

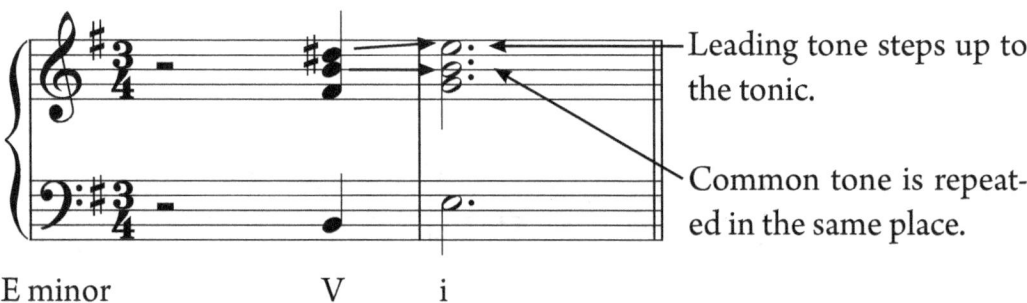

E minor   V   i

Writing the half cadence I to V is similar to writing the authentic cadence. There is a common tone between I and V. Try to repeat it in the same place and move the other voices down a step. In Figure 13.10 the common tone D is the top note of the chords.

Figure 13.10

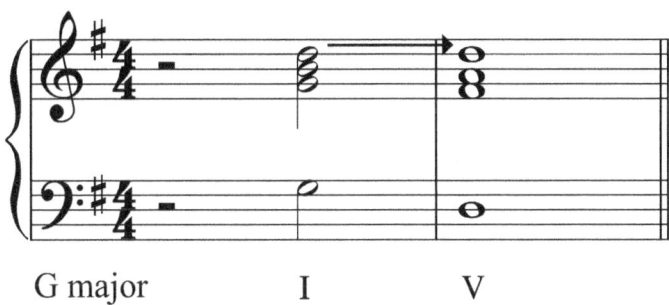

G major   I   V

The chords of the half cadence IV to V have no common tones. This cadence requires special voice leading. When writing this cadence, it is best to move the 3 upper notes in contrary (opposite) motion to the bass. The bass will rise a step, and the upper voices will fall from the notes of the IV chord to the notes of the V chord. In Figure 13.11, 2 voices step and one voice skips down to the notes of the V chord.

In this cadence, the bass steps up from iv to V (G to A). Do not write this cadence with bass falling a 7th from G down to A. This large melodic interval, a 7th, is not allowed here.

Figure 13.11

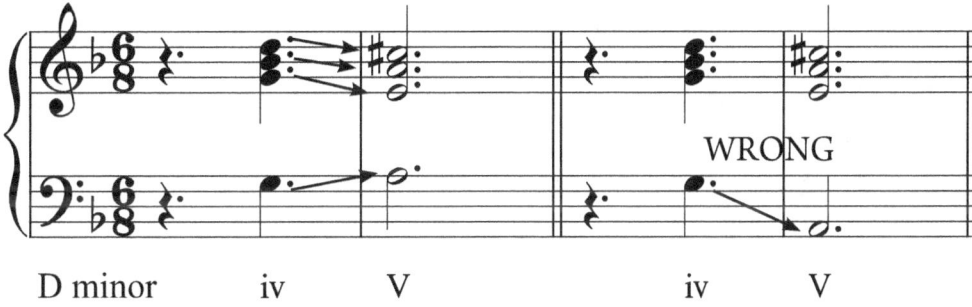

D minor   iv   V   iv   V

When writing this cadence, avoid writing two root position chords consecutively as shown in Figure 13.12. This is considered a mistake in voice leading and will be covered more extensively in the next book.

Figure 13.12

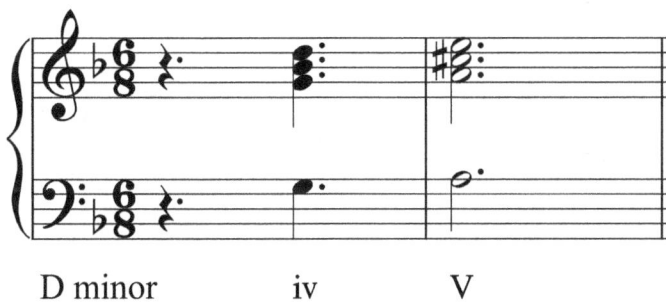

D minor   iv   V

1. Write authentic cadences in the following keys. Add functional chord symbols.

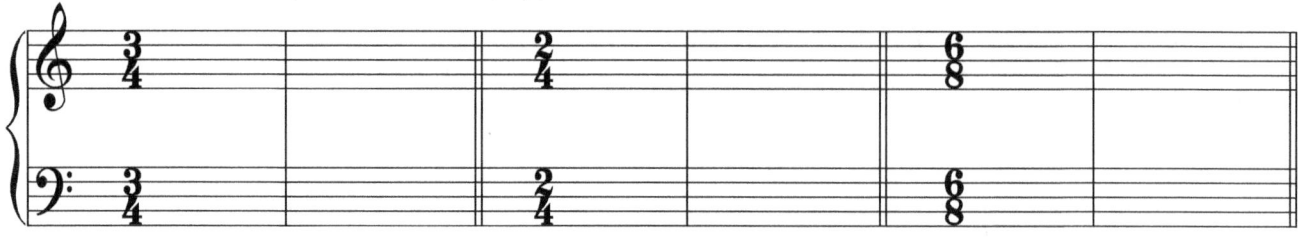

A major   C minor   D major

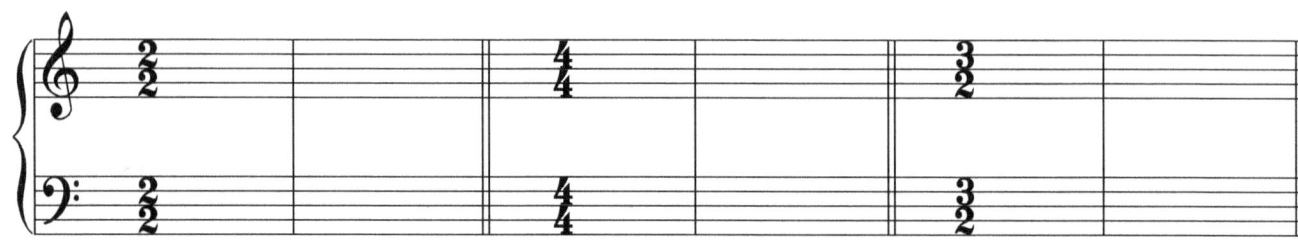

B minor   B♭ major   F major

2. Write half cadences using I (i) - V in the following keys. Add functional chord symbols.

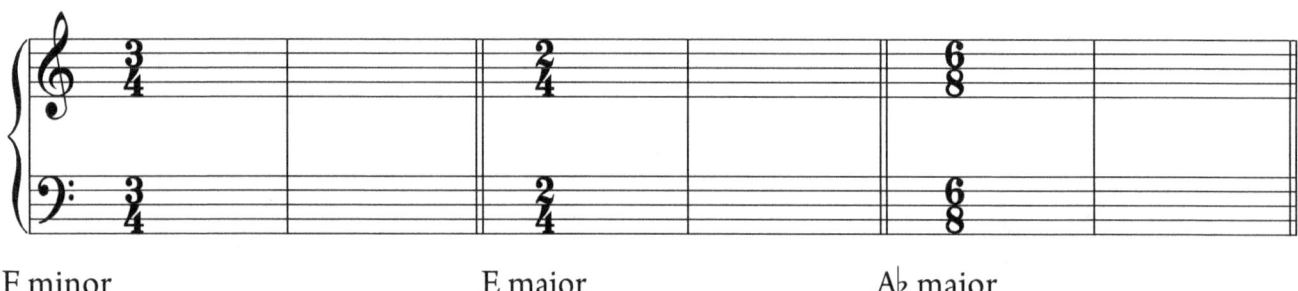

F minor   E major   A♭ major

3. Write half cadences using IV (iv) - V in the following keys. Add functional chord symbols.

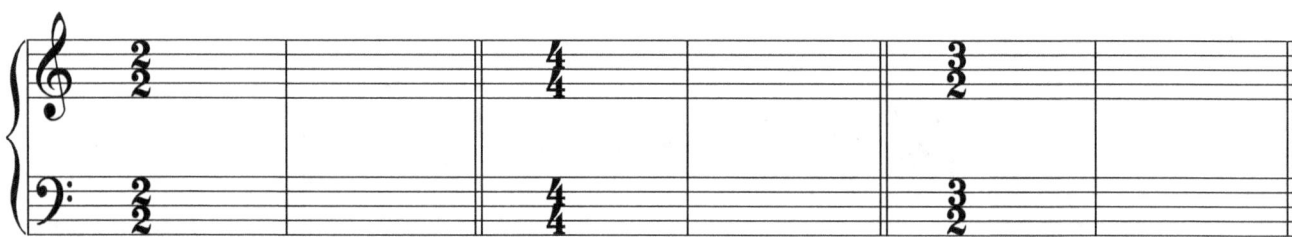

F♯ minor   C major   D minor

Writing Cadences at the End of a Melody

In this lesson, we will learn to write cadences in keyboard style below a given melody. It is important to remember that this is the melody and you should write the notes of the cadence **under** this melody. If you write above the given part, it will change the melody, and that is wrong!
Follow these steps for writing cadences:

1. Name the key of the melody (the melody below is in G major).
2. Write out the letter names of chords I, IV and V in that key (G major).
   - I   G B D G
   - IV   C E G C
   - V   D F# A D
3. Choose the two chords that will harmonize the last two notes of the phrase and create a logical cadence (authentic V - I, plagal IV - I, half I - V, or half IV - V). Here, an authentic cadence, V - I, is the only logical choice for the final melody notes A - G.
4. Write the functional chord symbols (V - I).

Figure 13.13

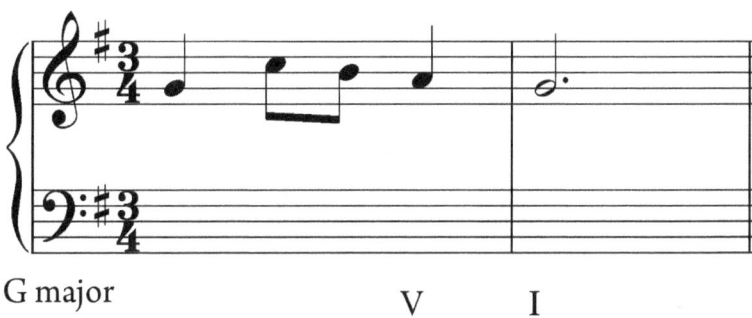

5. Write the roots of the two chords in the bass staff under the final two melody notes. Here, the bass notes for a V - I cadence are D and G.
6. Complete any empty beats in the measure with rests. In this example, the first two beats of measure 1 need a rest.

Figure 13.14

7. In the treble clef, add the remaining notes of the chords under each melody note to create a complete chord. Remember that in minor keys V will have raised $\hat{7}$. In Figure 13.15, it is not possible to keep the common tone (D) in the same place, and it is not possible to have the leading tone (F♯) step up to the tonic. This is common when the melody moves from $\hat{2}$ to $\hat{1}$.

Figure 13.15

Examine the melody in Figure 13.16 a). We have to determine if this melodic fragment is in E♭ major or C minor. It starts on C, but that doesn't mean it is in C minor. If we look at the three primary chords in each key, it will give us an idea.

	E♭ major		C minor
I	E♭ G B♭ E♭	i	C E♭ G C
IV	A♭ C E♭ A♭	iv	F A♭ C F
V	B♭ D F B♭	V	G B♮ D G

When we examine the chords in these two keys, there is only one cadence that fits with the last two melody notes (F - D). That is the half cadence iv - V in C minor. In E♭ major, F - D supports two V chords, and this does not make a cadence. This fragment is in C minor. Figure 13.16 b) shows the half cadence in C minor. Note that there are no common tones and the 3 notes of the iv chord go down to the 3 notes of the V chord. This is in contrary motion to the bass.

Figure 13.16

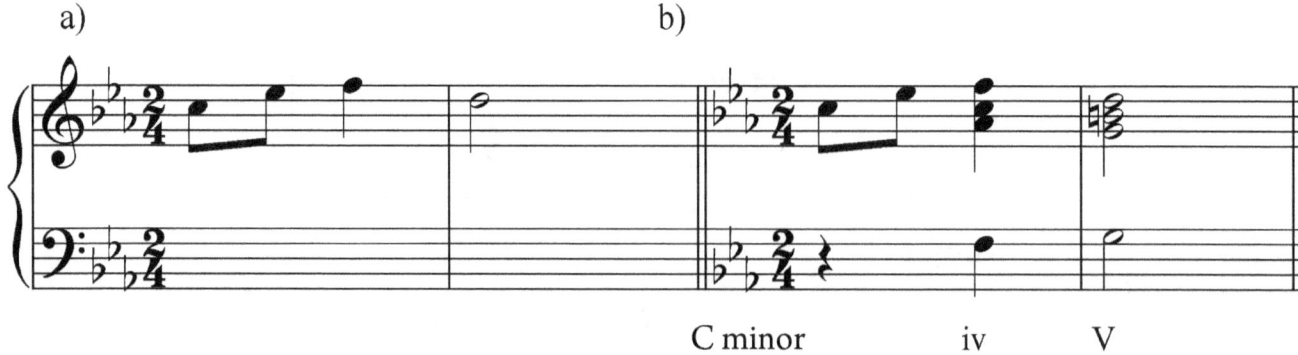

1. For the following melodic fragments: Name the key. Write a cadence at the end in keyboard style. Label the chords with functional chord symbols. Name the cadence as perfect authentic, imperfect authentic, or half.

Cadences

2. For the following phrases: Name the key. Write a cadence in keyboard style at the end of each phrase. Add functional chord symbols. Name the cadence as perfect authentic, imperfect authentic, or half.

Key:_____   Cadence:_____

Key:_____   Cadence:_____

Key:_____   Cadence:_____

Key:_____   Cadence:_____

Key:_____   Cadence:_____

©San Marco Publications 2022   Cadences

14

Transposition

Transposition Up by Interval

Music may be transposed from one key to another. Melodies in major keys can only be transposed to other major keys and melodies in minor keys can only be transposed to other minor keys.

A melody can be transposed up by a specific interval. For example, you can transpose a melody up a perfect 5th, or a minor 3rd, or a major 2nd, or any other interval. As an example, let us transpose a melody up by the interval of a major 2nd:

1. Determine the key of the original melody. You have to know what key you are starting in before you can determine the key to which you are going. The melody in Figure 14.1 is in E minor.

Figure 14.1

Robert Schumann
Album for the Young (Erster Verlust)

Andantino

E minor

2. Determine the interval of a major 2nd above E. Figure 14.2 shows that a major 2nd above E is F♯. The new key will be F♯ minor. The key signature of F♯ minor is three sharps. Minor keys can only be transposed to other minor keys.

Figure 14.2

The major 2nd above E is F♯

3. Write the new key signature. In this case, three sharps for F♯ minor. Rewrite the melody moving every note up a 2nd. The key signature takes care of the quality of the intervals in the transposition. In m.1 of the original, the leading tone D♯ is an accidental. In the transposition you must show this accidental in the new key. Here, the E is raised to E♯, the leading tone of F♯ minor. Copy everything from the original including the time signature, composer, dynamics, etc. Figure 14.3 contains the original melody transposed into the key of F♯ minor.

Figure 14.3

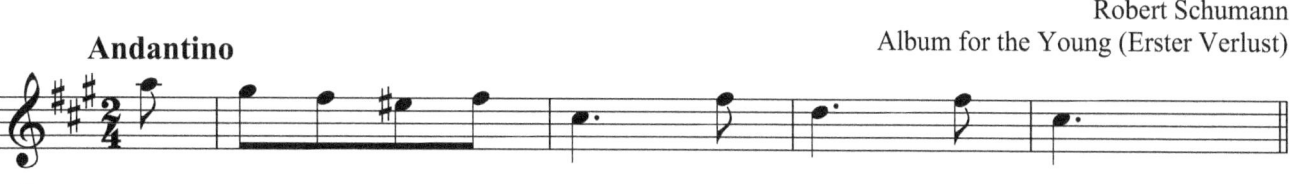

Robert Schumann
Album for the Young (Erster Verlust)

Andantino

F♯ minor

1. In the following examples you are given the original key. Transpose the tonic of these keys by the following intervals. Write the new key signature, the new tonic, and name the new key.

up a per 5th | up a maj 3rd

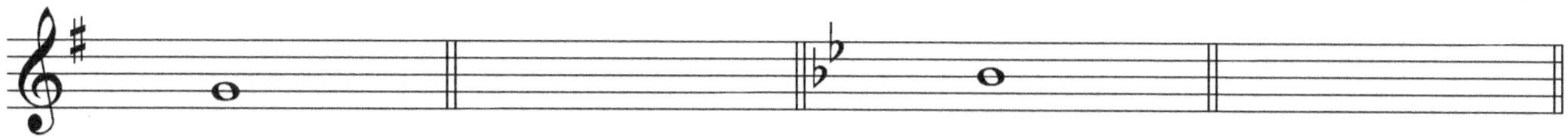

G major ______________ | B♭ major ______________

up a min 2nd | up a maj 6th

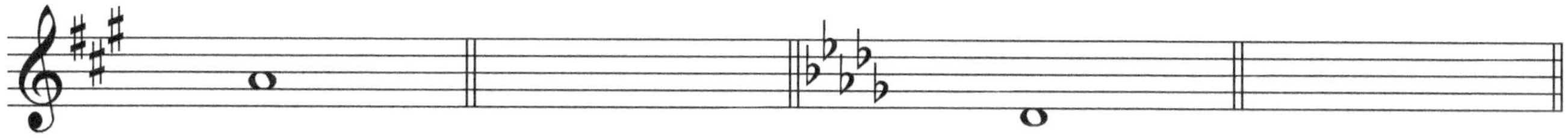

A major ______________ | D♭ major ______________

up a min 6th | up a per 4th

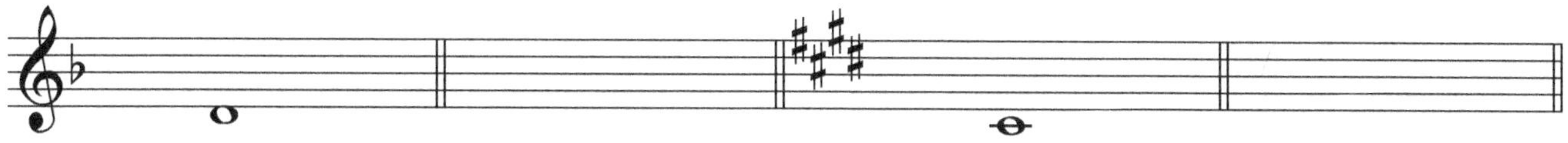

D minor ______________ | C♯ minor ______________

up a maj 7th | up a maj 2nd

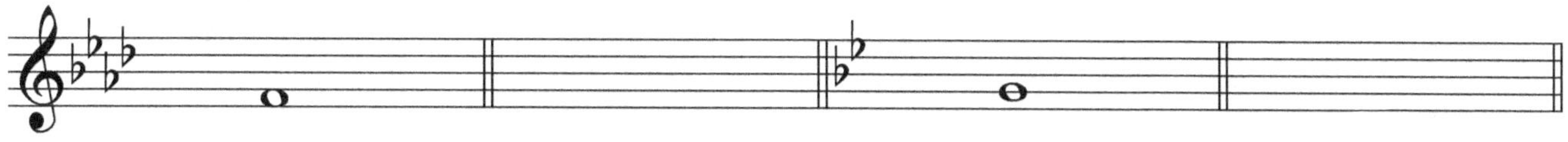

F minor ______________ | G minor ______________

2. Name the key of the following melody. Transpose it according to the given intervals. Name the new keys.

Traditional
Drink to Me Only

Key: _____

Transpose up a maj 3rd

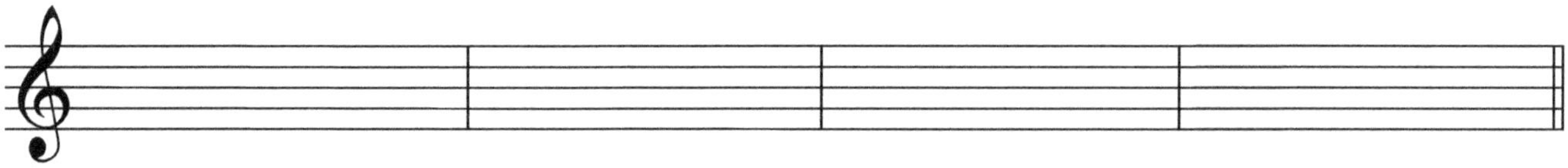

Key: _____

Transpose up a per 5th

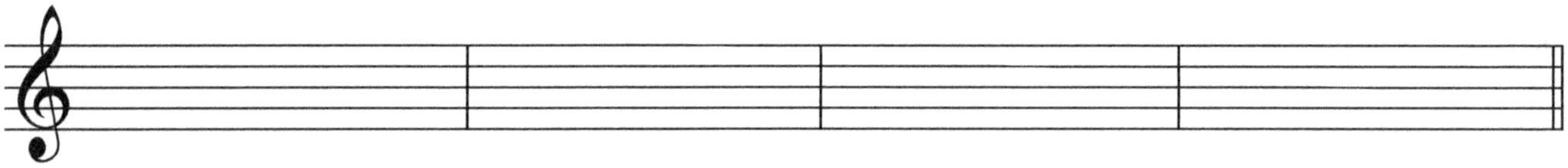

Key: _____

Transpose up a maj 6th

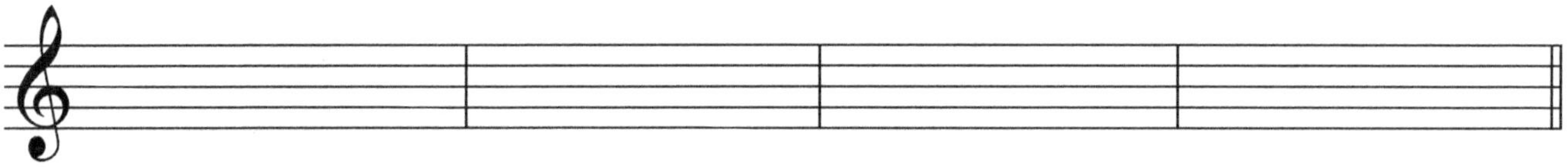

Key: _____

Transpose up a min 7th

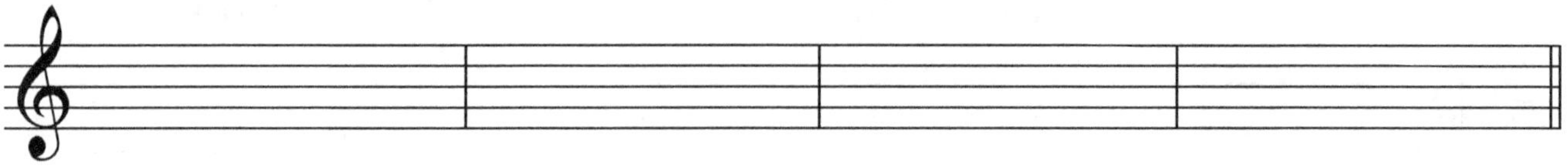

Key: _____

Transpostion Down By Interval

A melody can be transposed down by a specific interval. It is similar to transposing up. Here are the steps for transposing a melody down by the interval of a major 3rd:

1. Determine the key of the original melody. The melody in Figure 14.4 is in C major.

Figure 14.4

Johann Wilhelm Hassler
Minuet, Op. 38, No. 4

C major

2. Determine the interval of a major 3rd below C. Figure 14.5 shows that a major 3rd below C is A♭. The new key will be A♭ major. The key signature of A♭ major is four flats.

Figure 14.5

A major 3rd below C is A♭

3. Write the new key signature, four flats for A♭ major. Rewrite the melody moving every note down a 3rd. This melody has accidentals. Insert the accidentals where they occurred in the original. The first is raised a half step; the second lowered a half step. The original melody used a sharp and a natural. Using the new key signature, a natural and a flat are required to raise and lower these notes. Copy everything from the original including the time signature, composer, tempo, etc. Figure 14.6 contains the original melody transposed into the key of A♭ major.

Figure 14.6

Johann Wilhelm Hassler
Minuet, Op. 38, No. 4

A♭ major

1. In the following examples you are given the original key. Transpose the tonic of these keys by the following intervals. Write the new key signature, the new tonic, and name the new key.

2. Name the key of the following melody. Transpose it according to the given intervals. Name the new keys.

Anton Diabelli
Sonatina, Op. 168, No. 1

Key: _____

Transpose down a maj 2nd

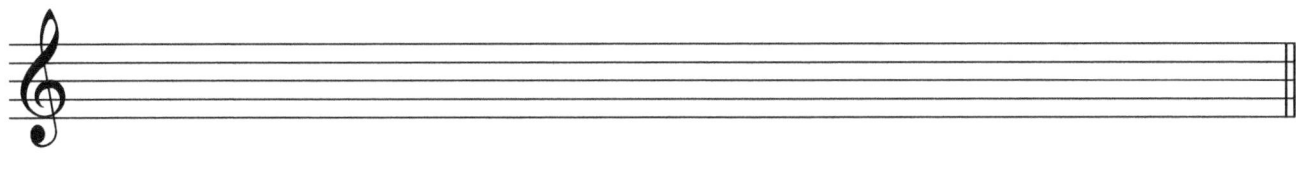

Key: _____

Transpose down a per 4th

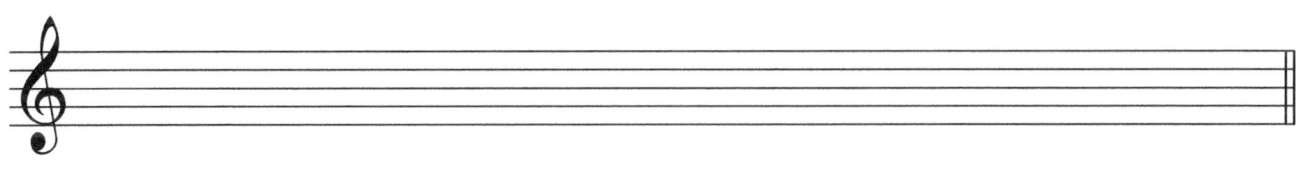

Key: _____

Transpose down a min 3rd

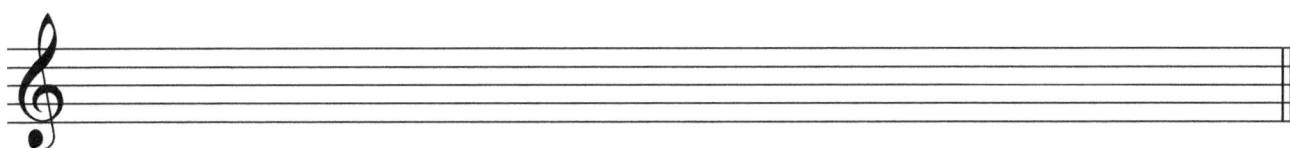

Key: _____

Transposition By Key

You may have to transpose to a specific key. The steps for this are similar to transposing by interval. Here, we will transpose a melody into the key of B♭ major.

1. Determine the key of the original melody. The melody in Figure 14.7 is in G major.

Figure 14.7

Franz Schubert
Unfinished Symphony, I

Allegro moderato

G major

2. The distance from G to B♭ is a minor 3rd. Write the key signature of B♭ major and move every note from the original melody up a 3rd. Copy everything from the original including the time signature, composer, tempo, etc. Follow the normal rules for stem direction. Figure 14.8 contains the original melody transposed into the key of B♭ major.

Figure 14.8

Franz Schubert
Unfinished Symphony, I

Allegro moderato

B♭ major

1. Name the key of the following melody. Transpose it to the indicated keys. Name the interval of transposition.

Ludwig van Beethoven
Symphony No. 9, IV

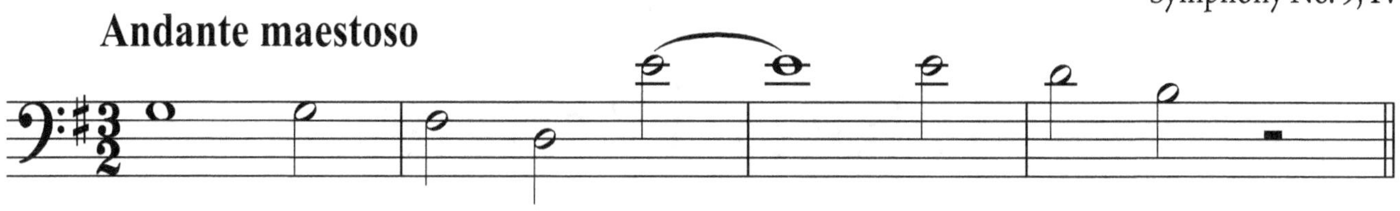

Andante maestoso

Key: _____

Down to D major

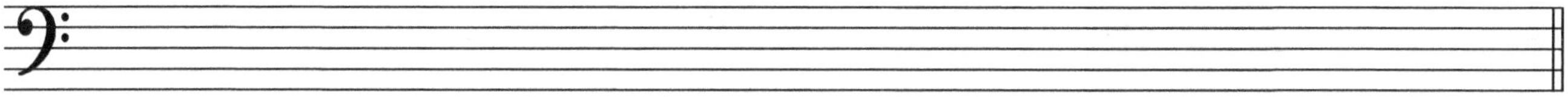

Interval of transposition: _____

Down to E♭ major

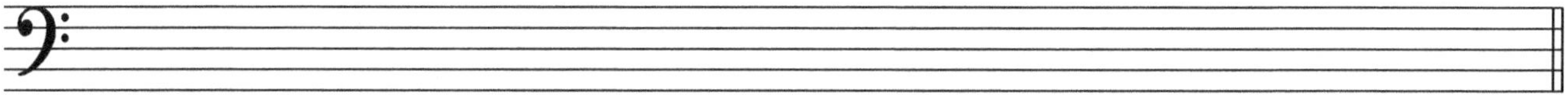

Interval of transposition: _____

Down to B major

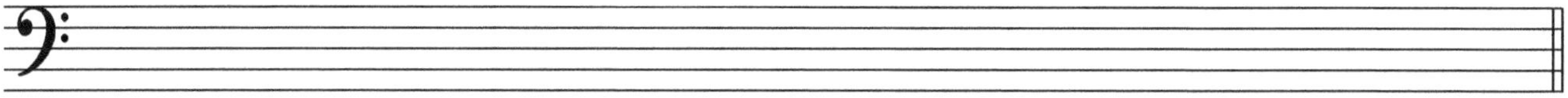

Interval of transposition: _____

Up to A major

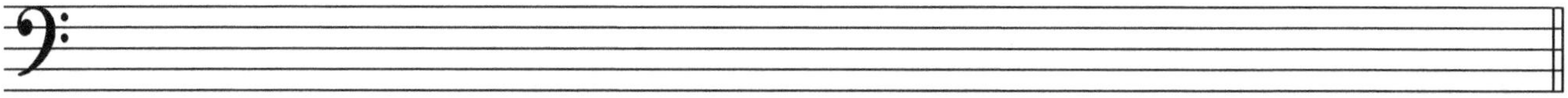

Interval of transposition: _____

©San Marco Publications 2022

Transposition

15
Melody Writing

Review - Implied Harmony

The notes of a melody can imply or suggest certain chords that may go along with it. This is called the *implied harmony*. Figure 15.1 contains the i, iv, and V chords in D minor.

Figure 15.1

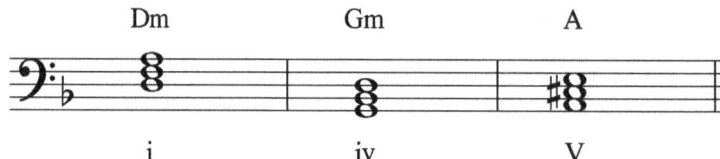

Chords can be used with a melody if they contain the same notes as those found in the melody. Study the implied harmony for the melody in Figure 15.2.
The D, F and A in m.1 suggest the i chord in D minor. This is the opening measure. Most pieces begin with the tonic chord. This helps to establish the key or tonality.
The G and B flat in m.2 imply the iv chord in D minor.
The A and C sharp in m.3 imply the V chord in D minor.
The final measure contains a D implying i and forming an authentic cadence with V in the previous measure.
Musical phrases must make harmonic sense and this includes implying a logical cadence at the end of the phrase.

Figure 15.2

Figure 15.3 contains the previous melody with the implied harmony realized in the bass clef.

Figure 15.3

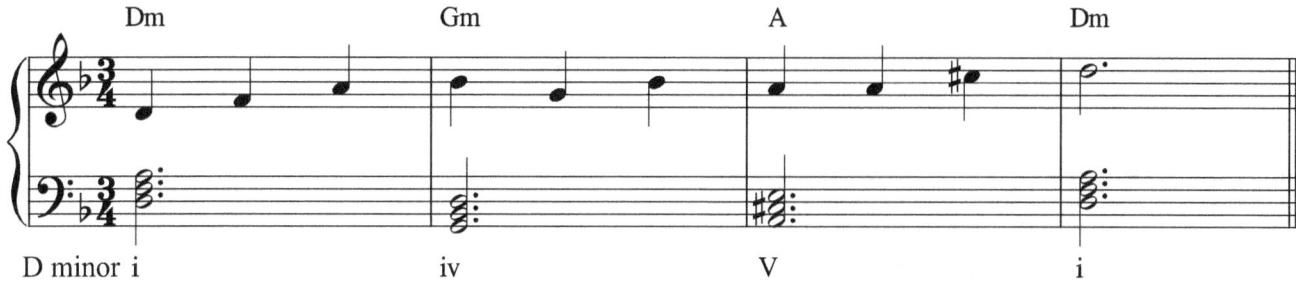

1. For the following melodies: Name the key. State the implied harmony by adding functional (Roman numeral) chord symbols.

Key:_____

Key:_____

Key:_____

Key:_____

Key:_____

Non-Chord Tones

A melody may have notes that are not part of the implied harmony. These are called **non-chord tones**. Non-chord tones always have a function or a reason for being. We do not write a note that is not part of the underlying harmony unless we can explain its function. In this level, we will study two different non-chord tones.

The Passing Tone (PT)

Non-chord tones are classified according to how they are approached and left. A **passing tone** is a non-chord tone that is approached and left by step. It fills in the interval of a 3rd. In Figure 15.4 (a), all of the notes are part of the implied harmony (I). They are chord tones. In (b), there are two notes that are not part of the I chord. These are non-chord tones. The notes D and F are not part of the I chord in C major (C-E-G). These two notes fill in the interval of a 3rd between C and E and E and G. Each non-chord tone is approached and left by step. The D is approached by step from C and is left by step to E. The F is approached by step from E and left by step to G.
When we analyze music, non-chord tones are circled and marked with an abbreviation to indicate their function. Here, PT is used for passing tone.

Figure 15.4

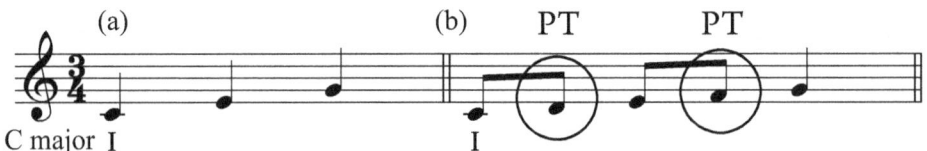

The Neighbor or Auxilliary Tone (NT)

A **neighbor tone** sometimes called an **auxiliary tone**, is a non-chord tone that moves a step above or a step below two common tones. It is approached and left by step. Figure 15.5 contains two neighbor tones. In this measure, the harmony could imply IV in C major (F-A-C). Anything that is not an F, A, or C is a non-chord tone. The two G's are not part of this chord. The first is an upper neighbor to the note F. The second is a lower neighbor to the A. They are circled and labeled NT to indicate their function.

Figure 15.5

Figure 15.6 is based on the melody from Figure 15.2. Here, the addition of passing tones and a neighbor tone add movement and interest to the original melody. Play and compare both.

Figure 15.6

1. For the following melodies: Name the key. Add functional chord symbols stating the implied harmony. Circle and label any non-chord tones.

Key:_____

Key:_____

Key:_____

Key:_____

Key:_____

2. Name the keys of the following melodies. Rewrite them adding passing and neighbor tones where appropriate. Add functional chord symbols stating the implied harmony.

Melodic Structure - The Parallel Period

A *period* is usually eight measures long and contains two four-measure phrases, called antecedent and consequent.

Antecedent and consequent phrases are common in music. The first phrase acts as a question, often ending on an unstable tone ($\hat{2}$ or $\hat{7}$), which requires an answer. The second phrase provides the answer and usually ends on a stable tone ($\hat{1}$ or $\hat{3}$).

The melody in Figure 15.7 consists of two phrases that are almost the same. The difference is the ending. The first phrase ends on an unstable pitch ($\hat{2}$). The second phrase ends on a stable pitch ($\hat{1}$). Since the second phrase uses the same melody with a slight alteration, the two phrases are labeled **a** and **a¹**. This type of melody construction, with two similar melodies, is called a ***parallel period***. In this example, each phrase begins with an anacrusis or pickup. This is common and helps create unity in the music.

Figure 15.7

Cadences

Phrases end in cadences. In Figure 15.7, the unstable pitch $\hat{2}$ at the end of the first phrase implies a half cadence.

The second phrase ends on the stable pitch $\hat{1}$, implying an authentic cadence. It is important that the notes at the end of a melodic phrase imply a logical cadence.

The Contrasting Period

The parallel period consists of two similar four measure phrases labeled: **a** and **a¹**. The labels **a** and **a¹** indicate the similarity between the two phrases.

The ***contrasting period*** consists of two differing four measure phrases labeled: **a** and **b**.
The melodic material in the second (consequent) phrase is different than **a**. For this reason, it is labeled "**b**".

Study and play the melody in Figure 15.8. There are two phrases: an antecedent and a consequent. Each phrase begins with an anacrusis. However, section **a** and section **b** differ. Section **b** uses the same rhythm as section **a**, but it contains new melodic material. This type of melody, with two differing phrases, is a contrasting period.

Figure 15.8

In Figure 15.9, the consequent phrase **b**, contains a contrasting melody based on a descending melodic sequence using rhythm from m.1. A ***melodic sequence*** is the repetition of a melodic idea at a higher or lower pitch.

Figure 15.9

You will be asked to compose the consequent or "**b**" phrase of a contrasting period. There are many ways to do this. The most important point is to try and hear in your mind what you have written. When you write an exam, you will not have access to an instrument. However, in the early stages, when you are practicing writing melodies, it may be a good idea to play them on your instrument to see whether you have written the sounds that you intended.

Writing a melody is more than creating patterns of notes on paper. It is about your creativeness and imagination. The most important features of a good melody are its rhythmic organization and the shapes produced by the pitches of the notes.

Here are some ideas to help you create good melodies.

1. When planning the rhythm of a consequent phrase look at the rhythm of the given (antecedent) phrase. Try to base your melody on related rhythms. The rhythm of the consequent phrase in Figure 15.9 is based on one measure of rhythm found in the antecedent phrase. Introducing an unusual or foreign rhythmic figure in the consequent phrase may make it sound like it does not belong to the complete period.

2. In Figure 15.9, the antecedent phrase begins with an anacrusis. The consequent phrase also begins with an anacrusis. This is very common and creates rhythmic unity.

3. A melody should have a sense of direction or shape. It may move to a high point or climax and then down again. Try not to circle around the same few notes.

4. Scalewise motion is good. A leap is the interval of a 3rd or more. Leaps are good for contrast, but try to avoid too many of them because the melody could lose its shape.

5. Avoid dissonant intervals. In major keys, an augmented 4th occurs between $\hat{4}$ and $\hat{7}$ and should be avoided. You can write a diminished 5th, but try to leave this interval to a melody note that is within its compass. Figure 15.10 illustrates a melody using these intervals.

Figure 15.10

6. The final note of the first or antecedent phrase is often an unstable scale degree like $\hat{2}$ or $\hat{7}$. This implies a half cadence. A logical cadence must be implied at the end of a phrase. End the consequent phrase on a stable tone, preferably the tonic. This implies an authentic cadence. A melody that ends on the tonic is very strong and reinforces the tonality or key. This final tonic note is often approached from below by scale degree $\hat{7}$, or from above, by scale degree $\hat{2}$. Study and play the phrase endings in Figure 15.11.

Figure 15.11

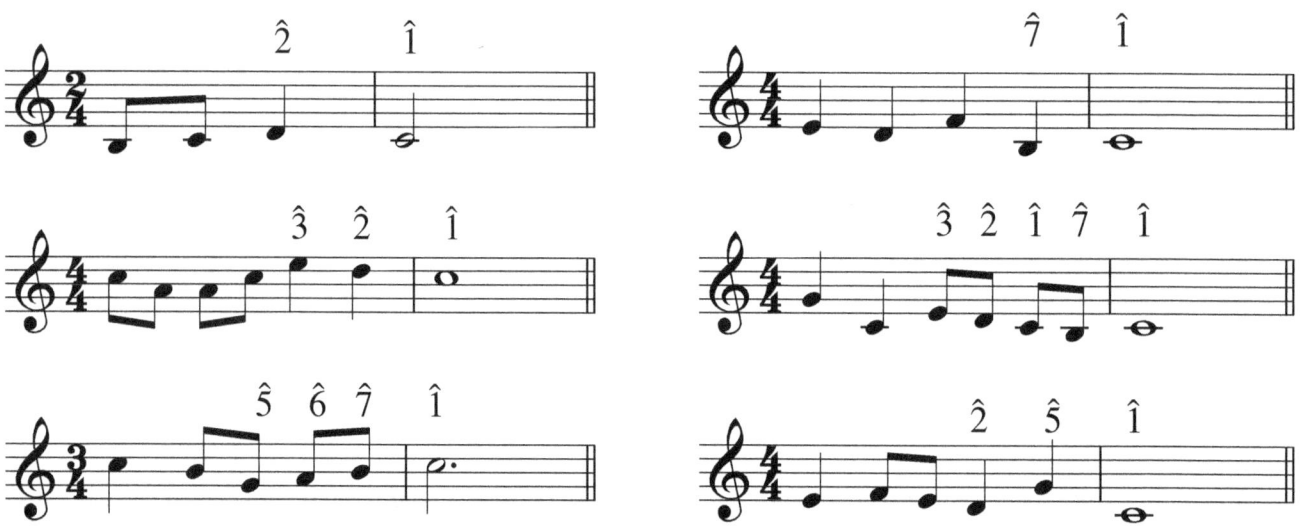

1. For following antecedent phrases: Name the key. Write a consequent phrase creating a **contrasting parallel period**. End on a stable scale degree. Mark the phrases. Name the implied cadences at the end of each phrase. Label each phrase **a** and **b**.

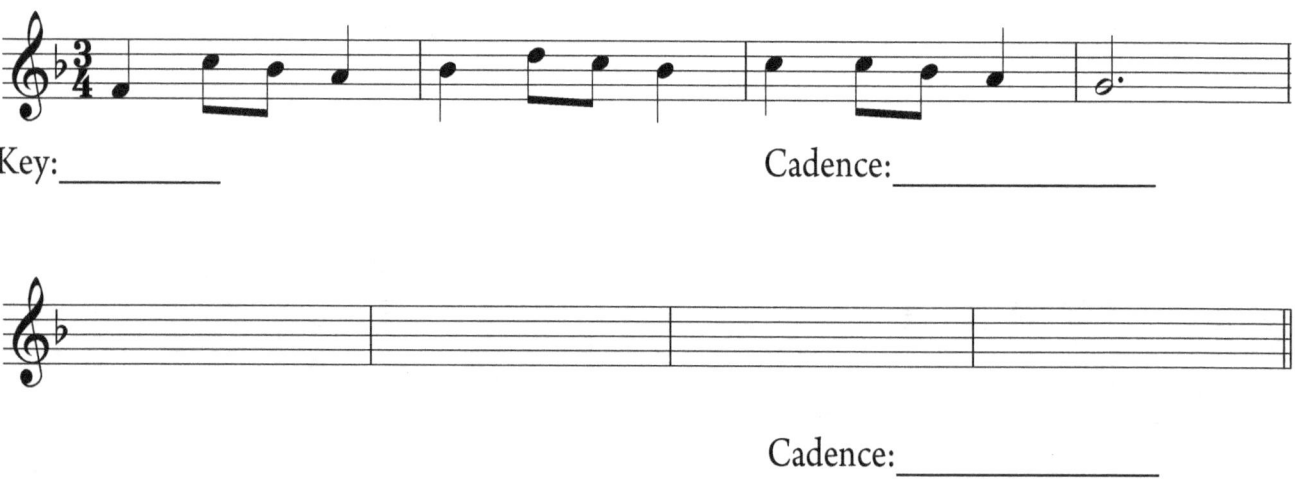

Key:_____   Cadence:_____

                                                Cadence:_____

16
History 3

The Modern Era (ca 1900 - present day)

In the Modern Era (1900 - present), composers followed traditional musical ideas but used their own creative approach. This resulted in freedom in all areas, including melody, rhythm, and chord progression. The development of audio recording technology, computers, and the internet was also very important to the development of modern music.

Music from the Modern era has a lot of variety. There are a number of different "schools" of composition. Many composers had their own way of thinking about composition, and how to compose in new and different ways. These new ways created new genres (types of music) that have names ending in "ism." Examples of these are impressionism, serialism, neoclassicism, expressionism, minimalism, and post-modernism. The Modern period also includes jazz, world music (music from non-European cultures), and electronic music.

Igor Stravinsky (1882 - 1971)

Igor Stravinsky was born in Oranienbaum, Russia. His father was an opera singer and his mother a pianist. Stravinsky began taking piano lessons at age 9. After high school, his parents convinced him to study law. One of his fellow law students was the son of the famous Russian composer Nikolai Rimsky-Korsakov. This connection allowed Stravinsky to take music composition lessons from the great composer.

Stravinsky became famous in the early 1900s when he wrote music for the Russian Ballet, including *The Firebird*, *Petrushka*, and *The Rite of Spring*. He fled Russia with the outbreak of World War I and took his family to Switzerland. He missed Russia during this period, and he composed music based on Russian Folklore as well as music influenced by jazz.

In 1920 Stravinsky moved his family to Paris where he lived for 20 years. Following the deaths of his wife and a daughter from tuberculosis, in 1939, he moved to the United States and became an American citizen. He died in New York City in 1971, having written more than 100 works.

Petrushka

Petrushka is a ***ballet*** by Igor Stravinsky. Ballet is an art form that consists of music, dancing, and scenery to convey a story or theme. Petrushka is composed for an orchestra with a large percussion section including a piano.

Until 1920, Stravinsky's works were deeply connected to his Russian heritage. The most famous ballet to build upon this Russian pride is Petrushka, composed in 1911. In this ballet, Stravinsky incorporated themes from Russian folk songs.

Petrushka was first performed in 1911 in Paris by the Ballets Russes. The story is based on traditional Russian folklore and features a puppet named Petrushka. Stravinsky's version of the story involves three puppets brought to life by a magician: Petrushka, a Ballerina, and the Moor. Petrushka, a wild and rebellious jester, falls in love with the Ballerina, but she only has eyes for the handsome, arrogant Moor. The Moor kills Petrushka in a duel, but Petrushka's ghost reappears to haunt the magician who brought him to life.

Petrushka is a complicated work that does not follow the conventional rules of tonality. Harmonically and rhythmically it moves away from traditional compositional rules by using unusual scales, polychords, and polyrhythms.

Petrushka has a pitch center (C), but it does not use the conventional pitch relationships that are seen in the major and minor tonal system. Instead, Stravinsky uses the octatonic scale as a basis for this work. An octatonic scale is based on alternating whole steps and half steps. In this case: C, C♯, D♯, E, F♯, G, A, A♯, C.

Stravinsky uses ***polyrhythms*** in Petrushka. Polyrhythm involves using two or more differing rhythms at the same time. For example, one musical line may be playing in 3/4 time, while another line is playing in 4/4 time.

Polytonality is also a feature of Petrushka. A polychord is a single chord made up of two or more different chords played at the same time. For example, if you take a C major chord and a D major chord and stack one on top of the other:

C major: C E G
D major: D F♯ A

The result is a chord that looks like the chord in Figure 16.1.

Figure 16.1

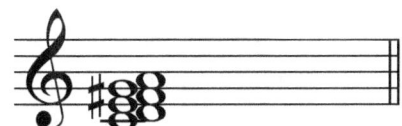

Petrushka does not have the traditional tonic/dominant relationship found in tonal music. A traditional piece of music in C might feature a lot of movement from C (the tonic) to G (the dominant). This tonal relationship is very consonant (pleasing). Stravinsky replaces the dominant chord with a chord based on the augmented fourth. The interval from C to F♯ is an augmented fourth, and this relationship is very dissonant (displeasing).

Petrushka moves between the two chords: C major (C, E, G) and F♯ major (F♯, A♯, C♯). The juxtaposition of these two chords represents Petrushka's bold and brash character. There are times when they meet, creating the polychord C, C♯, E, F♯, G, A♯ shown in Figure 11.18a. Since it is used so much in the music, this chord has come to be known as the "Petrushka chord." Figure 11.18b shows how this chord is derived from notes of the octatonic scale.

Figure 11.18

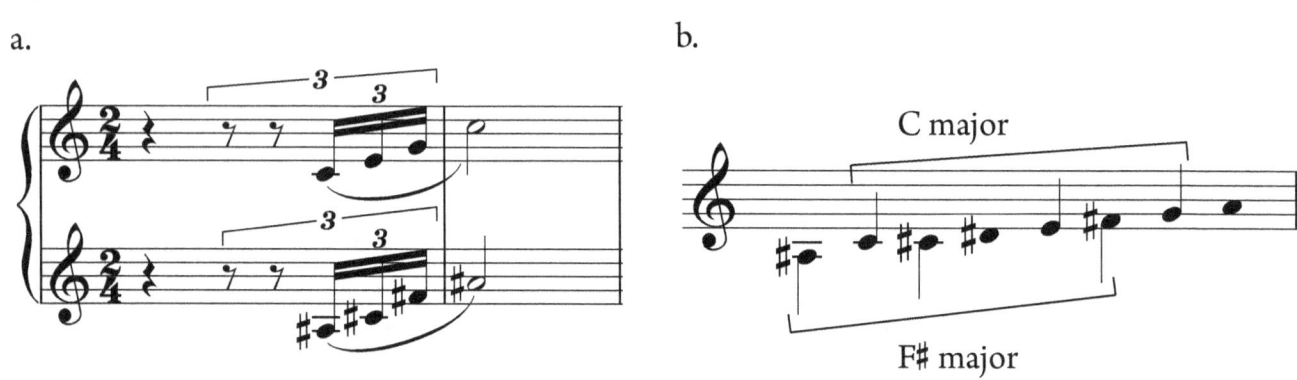

Rondo Form

Form in music is the way a composition is organized. The form is determined by several factors, including changes of key, when new musical material occurs, and when former musical material is restated.

Petrushka is in **rondo form**. In rondo form, musical material stated at the beginning of the piece keeps returning. This opening music can be called the ***theme*** or the ***refrain***. Between statements of the theme or refrain, there are ***episodes***. An episode is musical material that is different from the theme.

The theme, or refrain, of a rondo, is the first main melody or musical material that occurs in the piece. It will establish the key of the piece, and the theme will most often be played in this same key. Since it is the first material we hear in the piece, we label this part of the music the A-section.

The episodes usually differ in melody, in musical character, or in key from the theme. We label the first episode the B-section. For each different episode that occurs in the music, we use a different label, such as 'C,' 'D,' and so on.

In rondo form, the theme or A section will keep returning after every episode. One example of rondo form would be ABACA. The theme, or A-section, will always return after every episode.

The length of a Rondo varies depending on the number of sections it contains. ABACA and ABABA are examples of 5 part Rondo forms because they have a total of five sections. ABACABA and ABACADA are examples of 7 part Rondo forms.

Petrushka is a 7 part Rondo with its structure being ABACABA.

Duke Ellington (1899 - 1974)

Edward Kennedy "Duke" Ellington was born in Washington, D.C. on April 29, 1899. He was an American pianist, bandleader, and composer, most often known for his work with big band swing music. Ellington was a talented pianist but is famous for his big bands. These were orchestra-sized jazz bands that played dance music.

As an African-American composer working in Harlem, Ellington was an important part of the Harlem Renaissance, a period of artistic and intellectual production that took place in Harlem, New York in the 1920s. The greatest jazz players in history turned up to play with Ellington, and he wrote music to showcase their talents.

Throughout his life, Duke Ellington helped make jazz music successful throughout the world. He thought the term 'jazz' was not appropriate for his music because it was limiting. He referred to his music as 'American music.'

By the time of his death in 1974, he had composed thousands of original pieces of music including "It Don't Mean a Thing if It Ain't Got That Swing," "Sophisticated Lady," "Mood Indigo," "Solitude," and "Satin Doll."

To this day, Ellington is one of the most prolific composers and has personally contributed more to jazz music than any other person in history.

Jazz

Jazz is a music genre that has its origins in African American communities in the late 19th and early 20th centuries. Major features of jazz are improvisation and rhythm. Jazz musicians express themselves through ***improvisation***, requiring them to be inventive and create music on the spot. They do this by embellishing the melody or by changing melodies rhythmically. A key element of jazz is ***rhythmic syncopation***, which is when accents occur on the off-beat. Some jazz is ***polyrhythmic***, which is when multiple, contrasting rhythms occur at the same time.

Blues

Blues is a musical form started in the United States at the beginning of the 20th century. The blues are derived from spirituals, work songs, and field-hollers by African slaves. The first blues songs originated near the Mississippi River and were called the Delta blues. As African Americans moved throughout the United States, they took the blues with them and developed regional styles of this genre. Blues are the foundation of almost every American musical form in the 20th century, including jazz, rock and roll, hip-hop, and rap.

Twelve-bar Blues

12-bar blues progressions are organized into three 4-bar sections: four bars of the I chord, two bars each of the IV and I chords, and one bar of V, one bar of IV, and two bars of I (or one bar of I and one bar of V).

Figure 16.3 is the 12-bar blues in C. The right hand is based on the C blues scale.

Figure 16.3

Koko

Duke Ellington wrote *Koko* in 1940. This piece is inspired by drumming from African religious ceremonies Ellington heard in New Orleans. He wrote it for his big band which consisted of piano, drums, guitar, trumpets, trombones, clarinets, and saxophones. Koko's genre is **12 bar blues**.

Koko is divided into an Introduction, seven sections called choruses, and a coda. In jazz music, a chorus is one full statement of a song's form played through. In this case, each chorus contains the complete 12-bar blues progression. Koko is written in the key of E♭ minor, and all the choruses are in 12-bar blues form. Each chorus features different soloists and instrument combinations.

Listen to a recording of Koko on the internet, preferably a recording by Duke Ellington and his Big Band.

Musique Concréte

Musique Concrète was developed in the 1940s by French composer Pierre Schaeffer. It involves composing music based on recorded sounds. Musique concrète uses recordings of natural sounds, like water drips, the human voice, or musical instruments to create aural compositions. The sounds selected and recorded may be modified in various ways. They may be shortened or lengthened, played backwards, or varied in pitch and intensity. The completed work combines all of the sounds into one united composition.

Hugh Le Caine (1914 - 1977)

Hugh Le Caine (1914 -1977) was a Canadian composer and scientist. He received a science degree from Queen's University and worked for the National Research Council of Canada in atomic physics and developing radar systems.

He also focused on electronic music and sound generation and established a studio where he designed electronic instruments. He is considered a pioneer of electronic music.

Dripsody

Dripsody, is an electronic composition, and its genre is **electronic music**. It is an example of musique concrète, and was composed in 1955 by Hugh Le Caine. All of the sounds in this work are derived from the splash of a single drop of water. Le Caine used an eye dropper and recorded the sound of water drops falling into a metal wastebasket for 30 minutes before choosing the sound of one drop on which to base this work. The sound of this drop repeated over and over is heard throughout the work. He manipulated this sound in various ways:

1. He changed the tape speed. Speeding up or slowing down the tape created different pitches. In this way, he was able to assemble some of these pitches into a pentatonic scale.
2. He reversed the tape, playing the sounds backward.
3. He used four different tape loops or recordings of the water to produce repeated patterns or ostinatos.
4. He used tape delay. This was done by playing the sound and re-recording it at the same time creating an echo effect.

The piece begins with a single drop of water and increases in intensity by becoming more rhythmically active and dense until it climaxes in the middle. Then it gradually decreases in intensity and ends where it started, with a single drop of water.

Find a recording of Dripsody on the internet and listen for all of the features listed above.

Review 3

1. For the following phrases: a) Name the key. b) Compose an answer phrase creating a contrasting period. c) Write a cadence in keyboard style at the end of each phrase. d) Name the cadences.

2. Name the keys of the following melodies. Transpose them by the required interval. Name the new key.

Down a perfect 4th

Johann Sebastian Bach
WTC Bk. 1. No. 12

Key:_____

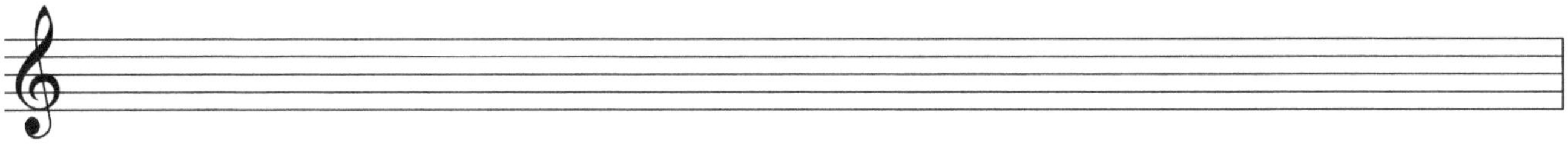

Key:_____

Up a minor 6th

Pyotr Tchaikovsky
Symphony No. 6

Key:_____

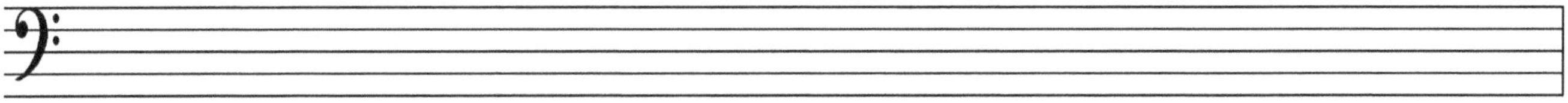

Key:_____

3. Name the composer and genre of the following works:

Petrushka
Composer: _____ Genre: _____

Koko
Composer: _____ Genre: _____

Dripsody
Composer: _____ Genre: _____

Etude Op. 10, No. 12 'Revolutionary'
Composer: _____ Genre: _____

Overture to a Midsummer Nights Dream
Composer: _____ Genre: _____

4. Match the Italian term with its definition. There are more definitions than terms.

quindicesima alta	_____	a) a passage for the whole ensemble
semplice	_____	b) time, *prima volta*=1st time, *seconda volta*=2nd time
sonore	_____	c) lively
sopra	_____	d) sad
tacet	_____	e) without
tutti	_____	f) play 2 octaves higher
volta	_____	g) with motion
volti subito, v.s.	_____	h) resolute, bold, strong
martellato	_____	i) heavy, play with weight
morendo	_____	j) sustained, play in a prolonged manner
pesante	_____	k) strongly accented, hammered
scherzando	_____	l) agitated
agitato	_____	m) majestic
dolente	_____	n) quiet, tranquil
giocoso	_____	o) sad, mournful
grandioso	_____	p) grand, play in a grand and noble style
mesto	_____	q) humorous, joyful
risoluto	_____	r) turn the page quickly
sostentuto	_____	s) dying, fading away
vivo	_____	t) sonorous, resonant; with rich tone
		u) simple
		v) above, indicates piano player crossing hands
		w) be silent, voice or instrument does not play
		x) playful

17
Music Analysis

The Primary Triads

The three most important triads in any key are built on the tonic (I, i), subdominant (IV, iv) and dominant (V). These are known as **primary triads**. Most folk music, sacred music, all of the blues, and a lot of rock are based on primary triads.

Figure 17.1 contains the well-known hymn "Amazing Grace." The entire hymn is based on I - IV and V.

Figure 17.1

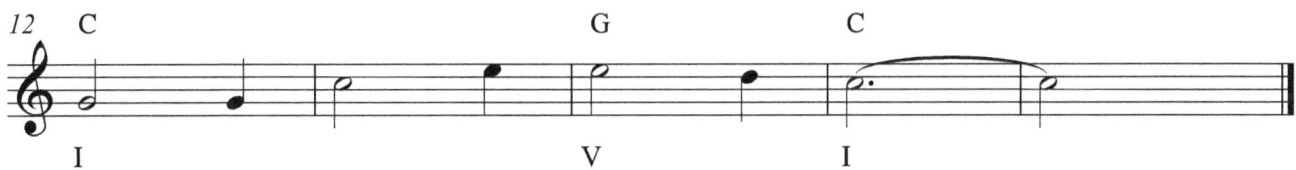

Primary Triad Functions

The Tonic (I or i)

The tonic triad in root position is the strongest chord in tonal music. It is important as a point of departure. Most music begins with the tonic and departs to other chords from it. The tonic might even be more important as a point of arrival. Almost all compositions end on the tonic chord. It acts like the home base for a piece of music. Like gravity, other chords pull towards the tonic.

The Dominant (V)

Some may argue that the dominant chord is the most important chord because of its pull to the tonic. The dominant actually helps us locate the tonic. The presence of the leading tone in the dominant chord creates an anticipation of the tonic chord. The leading tone has a natural tendency to pull to the tonic. Certain chords that contain the leading tone are referred to as **dominant function chords**. V is called the **dominant** because it is the most active dominant function chord.

The Subdominant (IV or iv)

The subdominant chord often leads to the dominant. For this reason, it can be called a **pre-dominant chord**. A pre-dominant chord is a chord that comes before a dominant functioning chord. Movement from chord to chord is called a **harmonic progression**. Movement from the pre-dominant to the dominant to the tonic is one of the strongest progressions in tonal music (IV - V - I).

1. Identify the following chords by writing the functional (Roman numeral) chord symbols under each. (I, IV and V or i, iv and V)

E minor

B minor

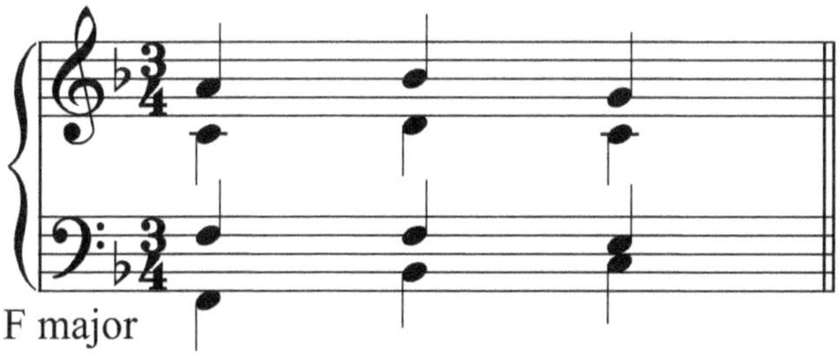

F major

A minor

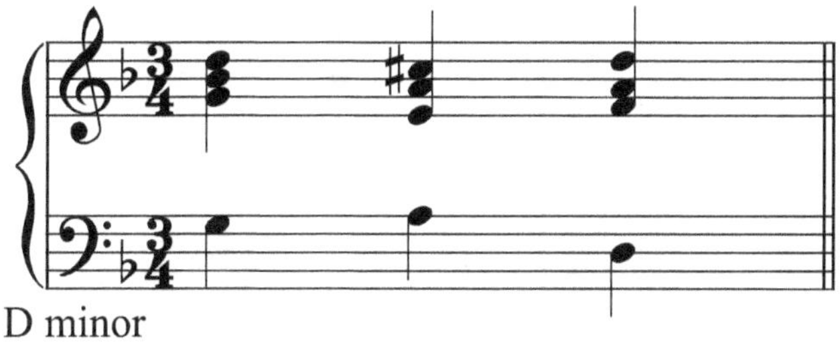

D minor

E major

G flat major

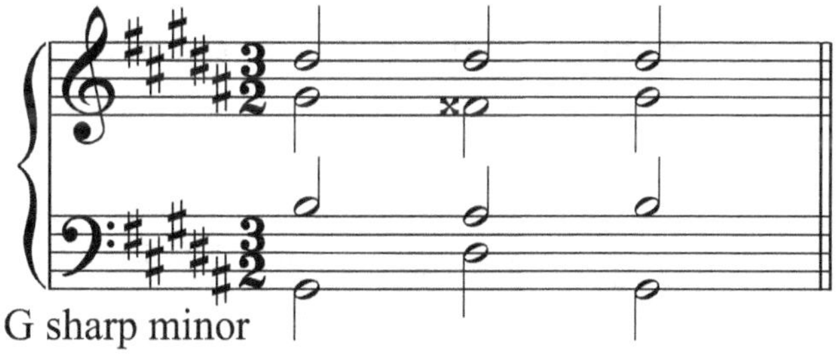

G sharp minor

2. Name the numbered chords as tonic, subdominant or dominant.

Wolfgang Amadeus Mozart

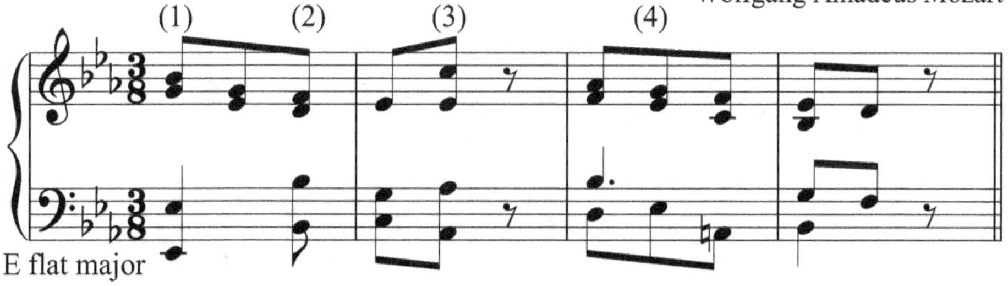

E flat major

1. _____

2. _____

3. _____

4. _____

Harmonic Progression

A ***harmonic progression*** is a succession of two or more chords. In tonal music, a progression is not just any two or more chords. Some progressions are better than others.

The most basic progression in tonal music is I - V - I. We call this the ***fundamental progression***. All that is needed to determine the key of the piece are the V and I (or i) chords. In tonal music, the relationship between the tonic and dominant define the key.

The first phrase of the Sonatina in Figure 17.2 consists of the progression I - V - I - V in D major. This phrase ends on a half cadence (I - V).
The non-chords tones are ***double passing tones***. These passing tones are written in 3rds. Double passing tones are usually written in intervals of 3rds or 6ths.

Figure 17.2

1. Write the functional chord symbol under each chord marked with ★.

Answer the questions about the following musical excerpts.

Felix Mendelssohn
(1809 - 1847)

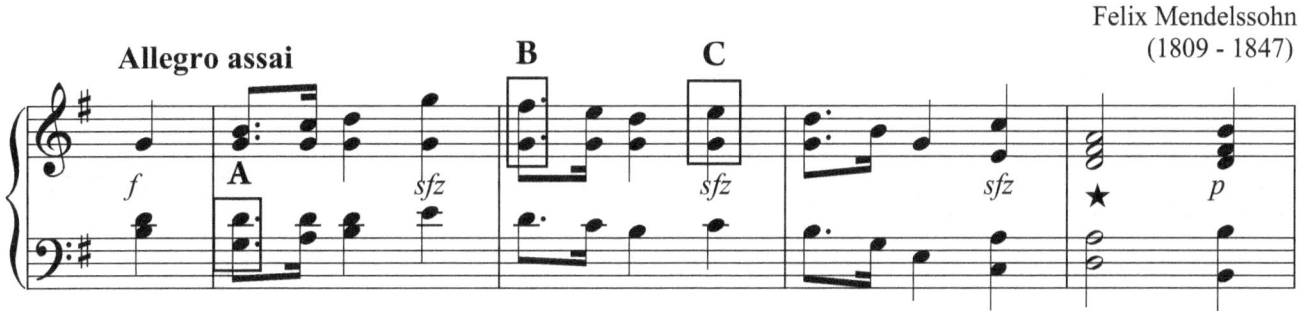

1. Who composed this music? _____

2. Name another composition by this composer. _____

3. In what musical era was it composed? _____

4. How many measures are in this piece? _____

5. Name the key of this piece. _____

6. Add the time signature on the score.

7. Add root/quality chord symbols at the chords marked ★.

8. Name the Intervals at A: _____ B: _____ C: _____ D: _____

9. Define: ***Allegro assai.*** _____

10. Define: ***sfz.*** _____

11. The cadence at E is: ❑imperfect authentic   ❑half   ❑perfect authentic

12. Why are there only 2 beats in the final measure? _____

©San Marco Publications 2022

Music Analysis

1. In what musical era was this composed? _____

2. What is the key of this piece? _____

3. Write the time signature on the score.

4. Name the chord at A: _____

5. In this key, the chord at A is the: ❏ tonic chord   ❏ subdominant chord   ❏ dominant chord

6. Name the chord at B: _____

7. In this key, B is the: ❏ tonic chord   ❏ subdominant chord   ❏ dominant chord

8. Name the non-chord tones at C: _____ D: _____

9. Define **Allegretto**: _____

10. Define *fp*: _____

11. Does the melody end on a stable or unstable chord tone? _____

George Frideric Handel
(1685 - 1759)

1. Name the composer of this piece. _____

2. Name another composition by this composer. _____

3. What musical period was this piece composed? _____

4. Name the key of this piece. _____

5. Write the time signature on the score.

6. This is an example of: ❏ simple triple time   ❏ compound triple time

7. The chord at A is the: ❏ tonic chord   ❏ subdominant chord   ❏ dominant chord

8. The chord at B is the: ❏ tonic chord   ❏ subdominant chord   ❏ dominant chord

9. The chord at C is the: ❏ tonic chord   ❏ subdominant chord   ❏ dominant chord

10. How many times does the tonic chord appear in this excerpt? _____

11. Name the intervals at D: _____ E: _____ F: _____

12. How many times does the leading tone appear in this piece? _____

13. How many times does the subtonic appear in this piece? _____

1. Name the key of this piece. _____

2. Write the time signature directly on the score.

3. This piece is written for a melody with piano accompaniment. This is and example of:

    ❏ polyphonic texture   ❏ homophonic texture   ❏ counterpoint   ❏ monophonic texture

4. In what musical era was this piece composed? _____

5. Name another composer from the same era. _____

6. Add the correct rest or rests to the voice part in m.1.

7. Name the interval at A: _____

8. Name the interval at B: _____

9. Name the interval at C: _____

10. Find and circle one leading tone in the voice part. Label it LT.

©San Marco Publications 2022

Music Analysis

Music Terms and Signs

Terms

accelerando, accel.	becoming quicker
accent	a stressed note
ad libitum, ad lib.	at the liberty of the performer
adagio	slow
agitato	agitated
alla, all'	in the manner of
allegretto	fairly fast, a little slower than allegro
allegro	fast
andante	moderately slow, at a walking pace
andantino	a little faster than andante
animato	lively, animated
a tempo	return to the original tempo
ben, bene	well
cantabile	in a singing style
col, coll', colla, colle	with
con	with
con brio	with vigor
con espressione	with expression
con fuoco	with fire
con grazia	with grace
con moto	with motion
crescendo, cresc.	becoming louder
da capo, D.C.	from the beginning
D.C. al fine	repeat from the beginning and end at *Fine*
dal segno, D.S. 𝄋	from the sign
decrescendo, decresc.	becoming softer
diminuendo, dim.	becoming softer
dolce	sweetly, gentle
dolente	sad

e, ed	and
espressivio, espress.	expressive, with expression
fine	the end
forte, f	loud
fortissimo, ff	very loud
fortepiano, fp	loud, then suddenly soft
giocoso	humorous, joyful
grandioso	grand, play in a grand and noble style
grazioso	gracefully
grave	slow and solemn
larghetto	fairly slow, not as slow as largo
largo	very slow
leggiero	light
lento	slow
loco	return to the normal register
ma	but
maestoso	majestically
mano destra, m.d.	right hand
mano sinistra, m.s.	left hand
marcato	play marked or stressed
martellato	strongly accented, hammered
meno	less
meno mosso	less motion
mesto	sad, mournful
mezzo forte, mf	moderately loud
mezzo piano, mp	moderately soft
moderato	at a moderate tempo
molto	much, very
morendo	dying, fading away
non	not

ottava, 8va	the interval of an octave
pesante	heavy, play with weight
pedale, ped	pedal
pianissimo, pp	very soft
piano, p	soft
piu	more
piu mosso	more motion
poco	little
poco a poco	little by little
prestissimo	as fast as possible
presto	very fast
primo, prima	first, the upper part of a duet
quasi	almost, as if
quindicesima alta, 15ma	play 2 octaves higher
rallentando, rall.	slowing down
risoluto	resolute, bold, strong
ritardando, rit.	slowing down gradually
rubato	flexible tempo with slight variations of speed to enhance musical expression.
scherzando	playful, play in a light-hearted happy manner
secondo, seconda	second, lower part of a duet
semplice	simple
sempre	always
senza	without
sforzando, sf, sfz	sudden strong accent on a single note or chord
simile	continue in the same manner as has just been indicated
sonore	sonorous, resonant; with rich tone
sopra	above, indicates piano player crossing hands
sostentuto	sustained, play in a prolonged manner
staccato	play short and detached
subito	suddenly

tacet	be silent, voice or instrument does not play or sing
tempo	speed at which music is performed
Tempo Primo, Tempo I	return to the original tempo
tranquillo	tranquil, quiet
tre corde	3 strings, release the left pedal on the piano
troppo	too much
tutti	a passage for the whole ensemble
una corda	1 string, depress the left pedal on the piano
vivace	lively, brisk
vivo	lively
volta	time, *prima volta*=1st time, *seconda volta*=2nd time
volti subito, v.s.	turn the page quickly

Signs

   accent - a stressed note

   **common time** - symbol for 4/4

   **crescendo** - becoming louder

   **decrescendo** - becoming softer

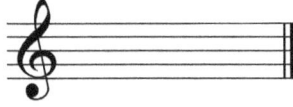   **double bar line** - the end of a piece

   **fermata** - hold note or rest longer than written value

   **glissando, gliss** - a continuous sliding up or down from one pitch to another

   **slur** - play the notes smoothly (legato)

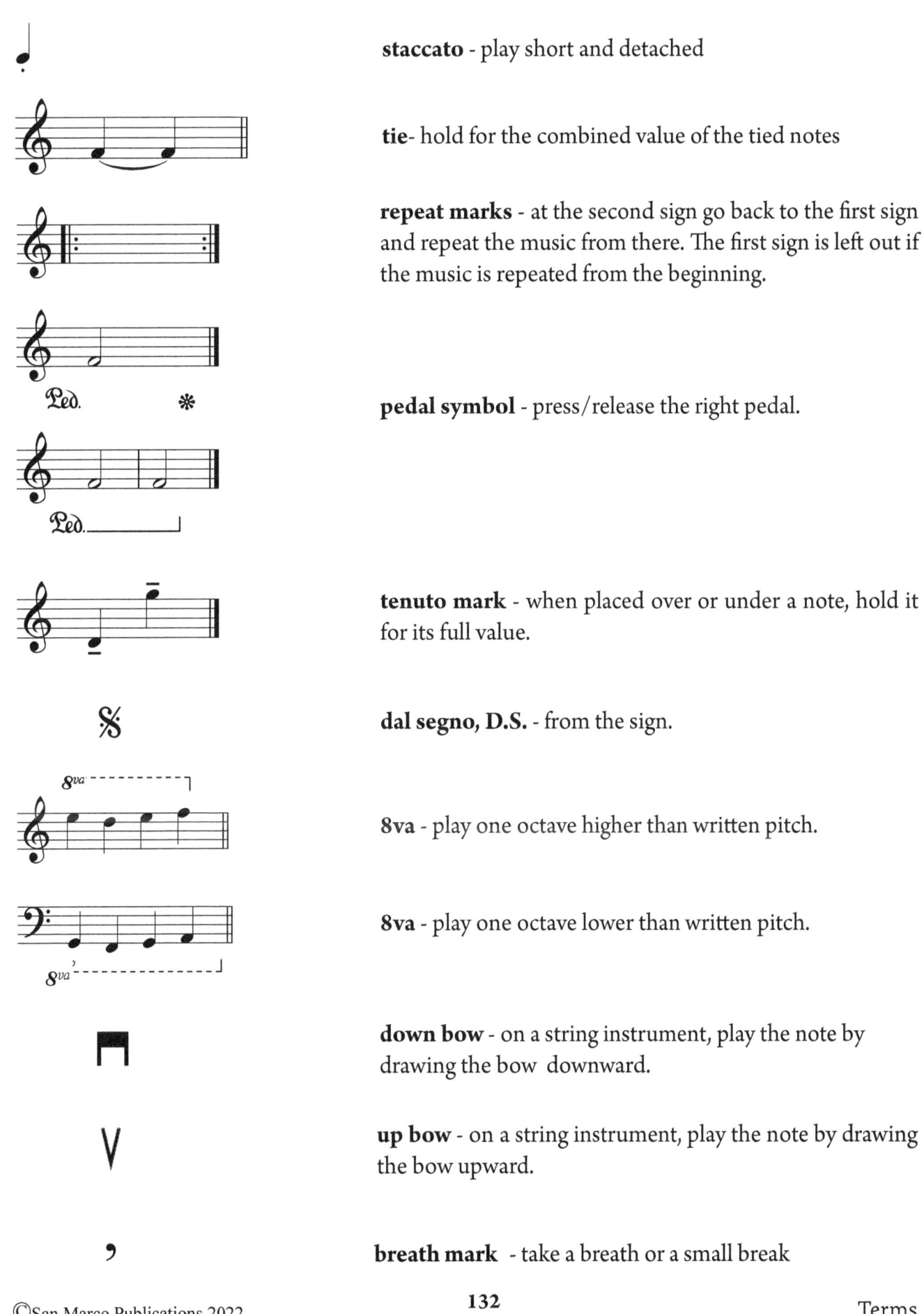

History Recap

Romantic Period (ca 1825 - 1900)

Overture to a Midsummer Nights Dream (1827)

Composer: **Felix Mendelssohn** (1809 -1847)

Key: **E major**

Genre: **concert overture** - A concert overture is a single movement concert piece for symphony orchestra based on a literary idea. A concert overture is considered program music. **Program music** is music that has a literary or pictorial association.

Composed for: **orchestra** - 2 flutes, 2 oboes, 2 clarinets, 2 bassoons, 2 horns, 2 trumpets, ophicleide, timpani, and strings.

Form: **sonata form** - This form consists of 3 sections: the expositon, the development, and the recapitulaion.

Etude Op. 10, No. 12 'Revolutionary' (ca 1831)

Composer: **Frédéric Chopin** (1810 -1849)

Key: **C minor**

Genre: **Etude** - a piece of music that focuses on refining and training a specific aspect of a performers technique.

Composed for: **piano**

Form: **Ternary** (ABA)

Modern Period (ca 1900 - present)

Petrushka (1910 -11)

Composer: **Igor Stravinsky** (1882 -1971)

Pitch center: **C**

Genre: **ballet** - an art form that consists of music, dancing, and scenery to convey a story or theme.

Composed for: **orchestra with a large percussion section including piano.**

Form: **rondo form - 7-part (ABACABA)** - a form where the main theme (A) keeps returning after contrasting sections called episodes (B, C).

Koko (1940)

Composer: **Duke Ellington** (1899 -1974)

Key: **E flat minor**

Genre: **12 bar blues** - Progressions in the 12-bar blues are organized into three 4-bar sections: four bars of the I chord, two bars each of the IV and I chords, and one bar of V, one bar of IV, and two bars of I (or one bar of I and one bar of V).

Composed for: **big band** - An orchestra consisting of piano, drums, guitar, trumpets, trombones, clarinets, and saxophones.

Formal structure: **Introduction, 7 choruses (each in 12-bar blues form), coda.**

Dripsody (1955)

Composer: **Hugh Le Caine** (1914 -1977)

Genre: **electronic music** - music performed using synthesizers, tape recorders, and other electronic instruments.

Composed for: **tape recorder, using the recorded sound of water droplets.**

Formal structure: **arch form** - begins with a single drop of water and increases in intensity by becoming more rhythmically active and dense until it climaxes in the middle. Then it gradually decreases in intensity and ends where it started, with a single drop of water.

Exam

100

10 1. Identify the following scales as: major, natural minor, harmonic minor, melodic minor, chromatic, whole tone, octatonic, major pentatonic, minor pentatonic, or blues.

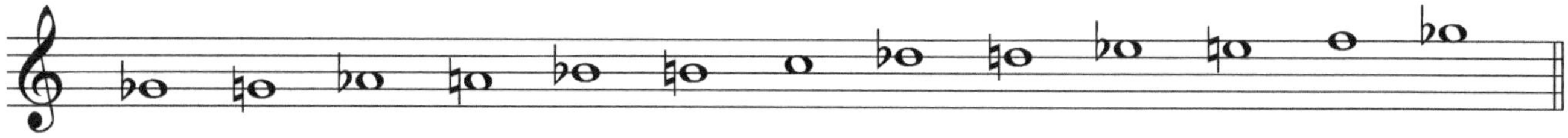

Scale: _____

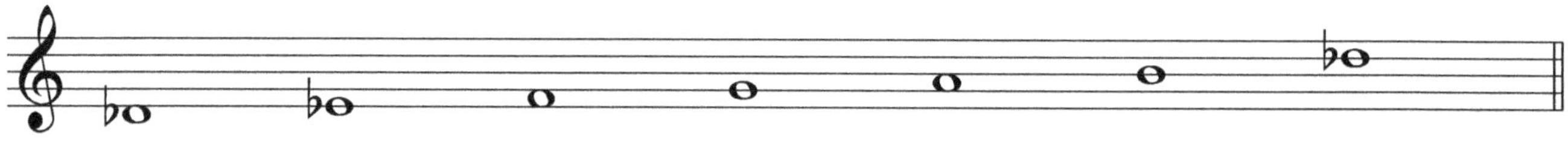

Scale: _____

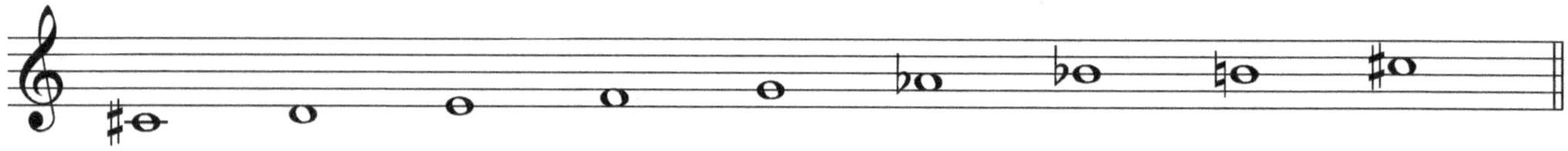

Scale: _____

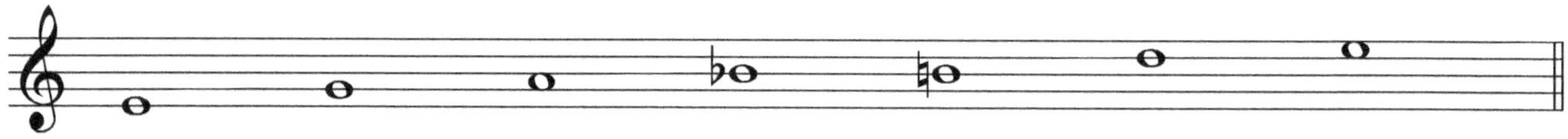

Scale: _____

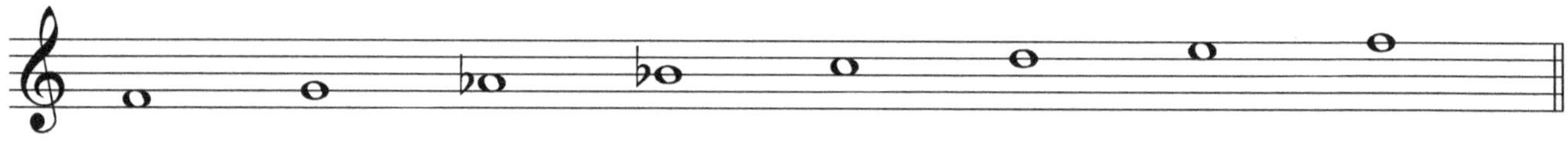

Scale: _____

10 2. Add rests under the brackets to complete each measure.

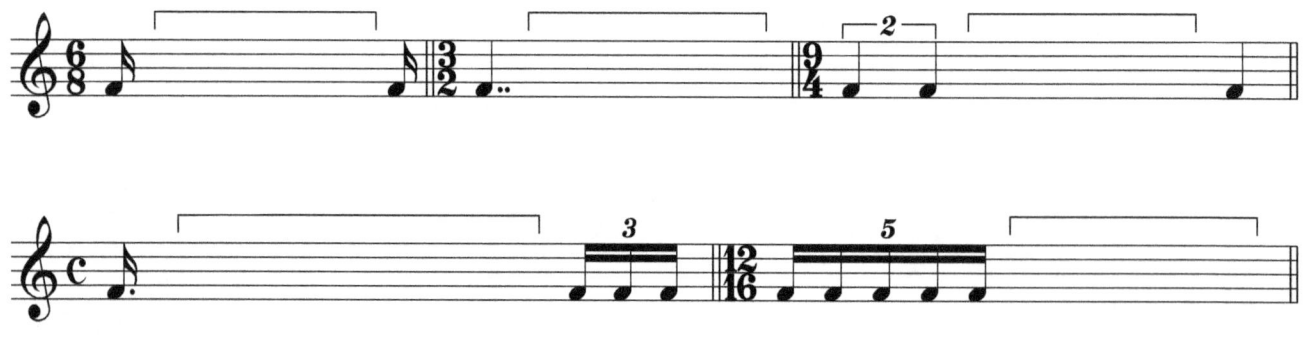

135 Exam

©San Marco Publications 2022

3. Write the following intervals above the given notes. Invert them and rename them.

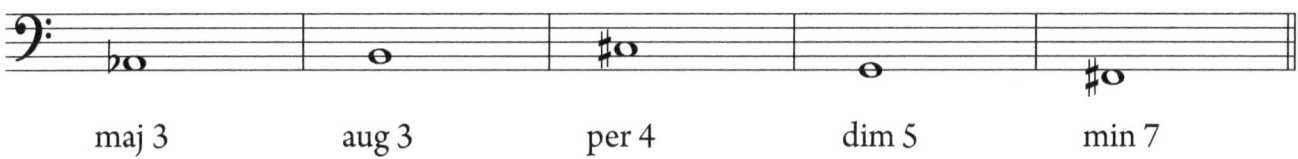

4. For the following antecedent phrase: a) Name the key. b) Compose a consequent phrase creating a contrasting period. c) Write a cadence in keyboard style at the end of each phrase. d) Name the cadences you have written.

Key:_____

Cadence: _____

Cadence: _____

5. Name the key of the following melody. Transpose it down a perfect 5th. Name the new key.

Johannes Brahms
Sextet op. 36

Key:_____

Key:_____

6. Write the following chords using the correct key signature for each.

| The supertonic triad of E♭ major in 1st inversion | The mediant triad of F♯ major in root position. | The leading note triad of G minor in 2nd inversion | The dominant triad of C♯ minor in 1st inversion | The submediant triad of A major in root position |

| vii°7 of F minor | V7 of D minor | vii°7 of B minor | V7 of A minor | V7 of B major |

7. Match the following Italian terms with their meanings.

____ *morendo*   a) playful
____ *semplice*   b) sad
____ *scherzando* c) simple
____ *pesante*   d) dying away
____ *mesto*   e) heavy, with emphasis

8. For the following cadences, name the key, identify them as perfect authentic, imperfect authentic or half. Add functional chord symbols to each cadence.

Key:_____   Key:_____
Cadence:_____ Cadence:_____

Key:_____ Cadence:_____ Key:_____ Cadence:_____

©San Marco Publications 2022

9. Answer questions dealing with the following musical excerpt.

Tobias Haslinger
Sonatina in C major, II

a) Name the key of this piece _____

b) Write the time signature on the score.

c) Name the chord at A: root _____ quality _____ inversion _____

d) Name the chord at B: root _____ quality _____ inversion _____

e) Name the chord at C: root _____ quality _____ inversion _____

f) Name the chord at D: root _____ quality _____ inversion _____

g) Give the function of the non-chord tones at E: _____ F: _____

h) Name the interval at G: _____

i) Give the term for the notes at H: _____

j) Define: ***giocoso***: _____

j) The cadence at I is: ❑ perfect authentic   ❑ half   ❑ imperfect authentic

10. Name the composer and musical period for the following compositions.

Composition	Composer	Musical Era
Dripsody		
Revolutionary Etude		
Koko		
Overture to a Midsummer Nights Dream		
Petrushka